H✝PE
1N NUM83RS

Holding Onto Promises Everywhere

HOW TO BE REMINDED OF GOD'S WORD EVERYWHERE YOU GO...

REVISED EDITION

GORDON WICKERT

Hope in Numbers

Copyright © 2018 by Hope in Numbers, LLC

No part of this publication may be reproduced, stored in a retrieval system or transmitted in any way by any means, electronic, mechanical, photocopy, recording, or otherwise without the prior permission of the author except as provided by USA copyright law.

Scriptures quotations marked (KJV) are taken from the Holy Bible, King James Version, Cambridge, 1769. Used by permission. All rights reserved.

Scriptures marked (NIV) are taken from the New International Version®. Copyright© 1973, 1978, 1984, 2011 by Biblica, Inc.™. Used by permission of Zondervan.

Scriptures marked (NKJV) are taken from the New King James Version®. Copyright© 1982 by Thomas Nelson, Inc. Used by permission. All rights reserved.

Scripture quotations marked (NLT) are taken from the Holy Bible, New Living Translation, copyright ©1996, 2004, 2007, 2013, 2015 by Tyndale House Foundation. Used by permission of Tyndale House Publishers, Inc., Carol Stream, Illinois 60188. All rights reserved.

The Holy Bible, English Standard Version® (ESV®) Copyright © 2001 by Crossway, a publishing ministry of Good News Publishers. All rights reserved. ESV Text Edition: 2016.

Scripture quotations marked MSG are taken from THE MESSAGE, copyright © 1993, 1994, 1995, 1996, 2000, 2001, 2002 by Eugene H. Peterson. Used by permission of NavPress. All rights reserved. Represented by Tyndale House Publishers, Inc.

Scripture quotations marked "ASV" are taken from the American Standard Version Bible (Public Domain).

Scripture quotations marked (NIrV) are taken from the Holy Bible, New International Reader's Version®, NIrV® Copyright © 1995, 1996, 1998, 2014 by Biblica, Inc.™ Used by permission of Zondervan. All rights reserved worldwide. www.zondervan.com. The "NIrV" and "New International Reader's Version" are trademarks registered in the United States Patent and Trademark Office by Biblica, Inc.™

Published by
Joint Ventures Creations, LLC | Glendale, AZ 85302
www.jointventurecreations.com

Cover design: Jesus Cordero
Editor: Trevor Santor & Sharman Monroe

Published in the United States of America

I dedicate this book to Jesus Christ, my family, my friends, my pastors and my youth group. Let's set this world on fire for Jesus. **"Never let the fire in your heart go out. Keep it alive. Serve the Lord." Romans 12:11 NIRV**

TABLE OF CONTENTS

Introduction — 1

Chapter 1 — 7
The Genesis

Chapter 2 — 27
Try it

Chapter 3 — 55
Renew It

Chapter 4 — 89
Use It

Chapter 5 — 123
Teach It

Chapter 6 — 141
Hold It

Testimonies — 168

Activities — 177

Games — 180

Birthday Bible Verses / Verse of the Day — 185

Jersey Number Bible Verses — 229

Dedication To My Children — 239

INTRODUCTION

We live in a world where hope seems lost; however, as believers, we have eternal promises from God that restore this hope. These promises are filled with power and are ready to equip us for the battles we will face ahead. The Bible has the ability to ignite a fire of purpose within every believer's heart from around the world to overcome every challenge and adversity set before them. God's faithful Word gives us the wisdom, strength, and courage to walk by faith and become all that God has created us to be.

The Word of God is a guiding light unto our feet for our journeys here on Earth. The Holy Bible is a history book, a love letter, and a map to salvation all in one to help us navigate our way through a broken world. It holds within it the playbook for people of faith to run the race specifically marked out for them. As you open up the pages of the sixty-six-book love letter from God, you will begin to hear the voice of Truth and feel the presence of our loving Father in whom you can place your complete trust. The inspired scriptures were written by human hands but were solely authored by God through His Holy Spirit. **"All Scripture is God-breathed and is useful for teaching, rebuking, correcting and training in righteousness"** 2 Timothy 3:16 (NIV). The Bible holds within it God's promises, truths, and sole mission for us all. I can't wait to share with you some of these promises and teach you how to see hope in numbers.

With God, the hurting become healed, the addicted are set free, the discouraged become encouraged, and the lost are found! The Bible is best explained using the acronym **B.I.B.L.E.** - **B**asic **I**nstructions **B**efore **L**eaving **E**arth. The Bible holds the foundational truths of this life, and if studied and followed, the results will be a blessed life! **"Keep this Book of the Law always on your lips; meditate on it day and night, so that you may be careful to do everything written in it. Then you will be prosperous and successful"** Joshua 1:8 (NIV). This book you hold in your hands will teach you how to keep God's Word on your mind and your lips as you hold onto His promises everywhere you go, day and night.

Before we begin, did you happen to notice the subtle details on the cover of this book? Go ahead and take another look. Did you see the handprint on the left and the scratches on the right? Those images represent the struggle of holding on to the promises of God as the world tries to rip them away. What you will also find, if you focus, is a subtle "Hope Wars" written between the hand and the scratches. I have it written this way because, just like in our own lives, we do not always see or recognize that we are in a battle for hope. It is a tug-of-war between you and the devil we all face in this fallen world.

Who will win this battle for the hope in your life? In the Bible, Jesus says, **"The thief comes only to steal and kill and destroy; I have come that they may have life, and have it to the full"** John 10:10 (NIV). The devil has come to rob you of your joy, peace, and rest in the Lord. Satan comes to destroy your life. On the other hand, God's Word is here to give you more life, joy, peace, love, abundance, and much more when we receive Jesus.

By practicing Hope in Numbers, you will strengthen your grip on the hope that is available to you through Jesus, and you will win this battle for hope! The devil is no match against God's Word. Like it says in 1 John 5:5 (NLT), **"And who can win this battle against the world? Only those who believe that Jesus is the Son of God."** I will teach you how to firmly grasp onto God's Word and His significant promises so that you can rip away any grip the devil has on your hope.

Introduction

From the time the Bible was originally written and distributed thousands of years ago until today, it continues to be the number one bestselling book in the world. Why do you think that is? It is because the Word of God has the power to heal, restore and save precious souls for eternity! **"Take the helmet of salvation and the sword of the Spirit, which is the word of God"** Ephesians 6:17 (NIV). With the promises, truths, and power of God's Word securely stored within the pages of the Bible and at our fingertips, it is in our best interest to open up the Word of God frequently and nourish our souls with the treasures hidden inside.

One verse can literally change the trajectory of your life forever! One promise from God can bring you from fear to faith! One verse held close to your heart can restore a precious friendship or save a covenant marriage from destruction. One truth can stop a panic attack from transpiring, prevent severe depression from settling in or release any built-up anger that is within your heart. Bible verses are the treasures of the soul for those who love God and want to pursue Him. Those who choose to hold Bible verses close to their heart and believe in them will become spiritually rich and blessed in their ways. **"Yes, a person is a fool to store up earthly wealth but not have a rich relationship with God"** Luke 12:21 (NLT).

This book will show you how to live a blessed life through faith by seeing Hope in Numbers. HOPE is an acronym that stands for **H**olding **O**nto **P**romises **E**verywhere. The convenient part about using numbers to memorize Bible verses is that the world has already done all of the hard work. When using something as abundant as numbers, you can remind yourself of verses everywhere. There are numbers all around you, on street signs, license plates, credit cards, and so much more! God is so good and mysterious. His treasures are hidden in every number

3

you see! Through the use of numbers, I am going to train you how to unlock these powerful truths and promises of God. You can find these timeless treasures and store them in your heart forever! Imagine, for a second, if you could be blessed every day, everywhere you go, no matter the circumstances. Is that something you would want for your life? Of course, you would. From the time you wake up until the time you hit your pillow, you see hundreds, if not thousands, of numbers daily. Phone numbers, jersey numbers, speed limit signs, time of day, calendar date, receipt totals, and monthly bills are just some of the numbers that constantly surround you. The world cannot see this hope, but you will start to develop eyes that can see the hope in something even as simple as numbers. **"'You have eyes—can't you see? You have ears—can't you hear?' Don't you remember anything at all?"** Mark 8:18 (NLT). Read this book to learn how Hope in Numbers works and how it can bless you everywhere you go!

The promises of God are out there in the world waiting to received by those willing to seek and find. This can be accomplished in a simple 5-step process which is the cornerstone of this book. You may be asking, who are these promises for? Let's look to scripture to share with you this foundational promise in the New Testament: **"And now that you belong to Christ, you are the true children of Abraham. You are his heirs, and God's promise to Abraham belongs to you"** Galatians (3:29). If you belong to Christ, the promises from God to Abraham now belong to you, to me, and to all who call on the name of the Lord, Jesus Christ. Here is the promise from God to Abraham: **"I will make you a great nation; I will bless you and make your name great; and you shall be a blessing. I will bless those who bless you, and I will curse him whoever curses you; and in you all the families of the earth shall be blessed"** Genesis 12:2-3

(NIV). Now this is exciting news! We will be blessed! All praise, honor and glory to our Lord Jesus Christ now and forever!

I believe with all of my heart that with this vision we will get God's Word back into our school systems, workplaces, communities, and the hearts of those we love. This book will teach you how to crack the code to memorize powerful Bible verses simply and easily. It will teach you how to transform your mind to see a number and turn it into a fresh revelation from God. **"This is the new covenant I will make with my people on that day, says the Lord: I will put my laws in their hearts, and I will write them on their minds"** Hebrews 10:16 (NLT).

I walk around every day blessed because I have received this wonderful gift from God: to be able to memorize His Word and see scripture in everyday numbers. **"Every good and perfect gift is from above, coming down from the Father of the heavenly lights, who does not change like shifting shadows"** James 1:17 (NIV). I believe God has blessed me so I can bless others by teaching them how to do this for themselves! That is why I have made it my mission in life to teach people how to see Hope in Numbers. To have a better understanding of this mission, it is crucial to go over Hope in Numbers' mission statement, value statement, and vision statement.

Our Mission

We are taking back this world for Jesus Christ by transforming every number we see into a timely, powerful, life-changing Bible verse from the Word of God that you can apply daily on the go so that nothing will be able to separate you from the Word of God.

Our Values

We honor the Bible as the written Word of God and the source of eternal truth. We seek to fully understand the Bible's context and apply Bible verses within the context in which it was written.

Our Vision

We see Hope in Numbers as a revolutionary way for people to walk out their faith by making it an everyday experience that reminds them of God's promises everywhere they go. We see future Christian families raising their children to see His Word in the numbers around them so they can know God all the days of their life and fall deeper in love with Jesus Christ.

To start our journey together, I'd like to share one of the theme verses of Hope in Numbers ministry. This significant promise from God from the book of Hebrews states, **"Let us hold tightly without wavering to the hope we affirm, for God can be trusted to keep his promise"** Hebrews 10:23 (NLT). Hold tightly to this book, God's Word, and your faith as we take this world back for Jesus Christ one number, one verse, and one soul at a time!

Turn the page if you are in…

CHAPTER 1 - THE GENESIS

I watched the time pass ever so slowly on the clock in the corner of my computer screen. It was just another day at work. I work as a fraud prevention agent at Discover Card to prevent criminal activity on people's credit cards. However, this job didn't fulfill my true life's work which was to help people discover Jesus and get their souls back by preventing the fraudulent activity of the devil. So I became a youth pastor at my local church to walk in that purpose.

On this particular day back in 2013, I was beginning to feel a bit overwhelmed by the time creeping by slowly on the clock. So, I did an unthinkable act— I grabbed a yellow sticky note and wrote "Matthew 6:33" on it and plopped it right over the clock of my computer screen. Boom. anxiety gone!

Now, instead of the time on the clock working against me and keeping me in shackles until my shift was over, I was set free and revived by God's promise. Matthew 6:33 Is my life verse and I continue to try and live out every day. So, I thought it was fitting to have it at my workstation. What happened next changed how I saw numbers and God's Word forever.

Minutes later, my manager walked up to my workstation and said, "Gordon, I know that's a Bible verse on your computer, and I need you to take it down." I was in awe because as I looked around, everybody else in the office had little reminders and trinkets of what they loved and followed around their workstations. Why couldn't I express what I love and have a Bible verse up? That is the world we live in today.

Here is what I did next: a small, rebellious act for the Lord; I took a deep breath, took the sticky note, and ripped off the part that said "Matthew" and left the reference "6:33" and I placed it back over the time on my computer screen. I was a fraud agent and worked with numbers all day, so my manager couldn't say anything more about it because it was just a number. I was astonished because I could still see God's promise in it! This memorization technique launched a new way of life for me and the start of my ministry. **"You intended to harm me, but God intended it all for good. He brought me to this position so I could save the lives of many people"** Genesis 50:20 (NLT). My manager at Discover Card aided me in discovering this marvelous gift that I believe will soon transform and bless many people. So, for that, I thank you, sir!

When I went home from work that day, things really started to get strange and exciting! I began to see the number '633' in random places in and around my home. Do you ever feel like when you shop for a particular car, you start to recognize it everywhere you go? Or when you buy a brand of clothing or shoe, and then you start seeing other people wearing it. This same concept was happening here, but with a number and God's Word!

Here is what happened. I pulled into my driveway and noticed that my neighbor's license plate number had '633' in it, as plain as day! Then I walked inside my house, and the clock read 6:33 p.m. And if that wasn't enough confirmation already, as I was checking my mail, I noticed that the number '633' was divinely placed in the zip code of my home address!

In this moment, I knew God was up to something. The wheels in my head started to spin. Could this be? Here I was reminded of a promise that Jesus spoke over 2,000 years ago from the book of Matthew by randomly seeing the number '633' out in the world. Here was my big 'aha moment.' I wondered how many other verses I could seek and find out in the world. That is when God revealed to me the hidden promises in every number. **"Ask and it will be given to you; seek and you will find; knock and the door will be opened to you"** Matthew 7:7 (NIV). God was making it my mission field to create a fun, new way to memorize Bible verses and see them out in the world!

Every Hour of Every Day

After discovering the possibility of seeing God's word in every number, Jesus gave me this cool thought. People in this world love knowing the Zodiac sign that goes with their birthdate. So, I wondered if there was a Bible verse for everyone's birthday that corresponds with the date and gives them real hope instead of made up, wishful thinking of a Zodiac sign. Sorry if you are one to believe in Zodiac signs, but God promises real hope through His Word!

I began this journey to find a significant Bible verse and promise that went with every day of the year. I call it your Birthday Bible Verse! I started with January 1 or 1/1 and wanted to get through December 31 or 12/31. It took about a year of searching through all sixty-six books for the best promises and truths with every date.

I think God has a funny sense of humor because when it came time to look up my Birthday Bible Verse for September 21st (9/21), I put 9:21 into the search function on the YouVersion Bible app, and the first verse I saw came from the book of Genesis. **"One day he drank some wine he had made, and he became drunk and lay naked inside his tent"** Genesis 9:21 (NLT). This verse was about Noah and how one day, maybe it was his birthday too, he got drunk and passed out in his birthday suit. Having this verse show up was hilarious if you knew me personally because I'm thirty-five years old and have made it my life's goal never to taste or drink alcohol.

Of course, that's not the verse I chose for my Birthday Bible Verse. What I did choose was 1 Corinthians 9:21 (NIV): **"To those not having the law I became like one not having the law (though I am not free from God's law but am under Christ's law), so as to win those not having the law."** This Bible verse fits me perfectly because I feel like I live out this verse as best as I can when I am around unbelievers. I am hoping your Birthday Bible verse will fit you perfectly too! If you haven't already, go ahead and look in the back of this book. Find your Birthday Bible Verse and see if it speaks to you as it does for me and many others!

After I discovered a Bible verse for every date, I thought to myself: I wonder if there is a Bible verse for every time of the day. So, I made it my mission to find a Bible verse for every time of the day. That way, when you look at the clock, you could be blessed with a timely word from God and not be stressed. Time would no longer be against you, but it would be for you!

The journey of finding these Bible verses for every day was going pretty smoothly. Every night I would spend thirty minutes to an hour looking through every book of the Bible for the best verse I could find. I hoped and prayed this idea would work and be a blessing to others. As I neared the end of my journey, I was getting a little bit anxious. Here's why: When I started with 1:1, I had sixty-six books to choose from because every book had at least one verse. But when I got to the higher times of the day, I ran out of options for powerful and inspiring Bible verses. But read how big and faithful our God is! Following, is just another confirmation story of how I know this idea came from God.

I was in the final stretch. Searching for verses in the high 12:50s, I was running out of options for books of the Bible. There are not a lot of books in the Bible with twelve chapters and fifty verses in them. I got to the last time: 12:59 am/pm, and I put the number into the search function in my Bible app. Seriously, there was only one Bible verse that came up! One book in the entire Bible that contains twelve chapters and fifty-nine verses! Can anybody guess what book it was?

If you guessed the book of Luke, you are right! Here's the crazy part. For fun, I searched to see if there was a verse higher than 12:59 in the Bible. I typed in 12:60 to find out there was not a single verse for 12:60 written in any of the sixty-six books of the Bible! I saw this as complete confirmation that the Lord was for this idea. He will use this new perspective to bless the world every minute of each day! The world would read this story and call it a COINCIDENCE, but as believers in Christ, we can call it EVIDENCE of our faithful God! **"The Lord himself goes before you and will be with you; he will never leave you nor forsake you. Do not be afraid; do not be discouraged"** Deuteronomy 31:8 (NIV).

Naming the Ministry

After discovering this ability to see Bible verses in numbers, I wanted to call it something unique so that I could tell people about it and teach others how to do it too. I wanted so much for others to know about this and experience the blessings and joy I was experiencing from being reminded of God's promises. I was so amazed at how God continued to speak to me through His Word through numbers. I just had to get this out to the world!

I started to brainstorm ways to describe this newfound ability to people. I felt like I had a superpower, like those superheroes in the movies. But instead of made-up scenarios of saving the world, this superpower pointed people to the only real Hero who can truly save the world, and His name is Jesus

Christ! **"I have come into the world as light, so that whoever believes in me may not remain in darkness. If anyone hears my words and does not keep them, I do not judge him; for I did not come to judge the world but to save the world"** John 12:46-47 (ESV).

This powerful ability to see God's Word everywhere you go is something you can take possession! I encourage you- read this book in its entirety and discover for yourself how you can receive the gift of seeing Hope in Numbers. Pray for this gift, and I know you will be blessed when you do. **"But you will receive power when the Holy Spirit comes upon you. And you will be my witnesses, telling people about me everywhere—in Jerusalem, throughout Judea, in Samaria, and to the ends of the earth"** Acts 1:8 (NLT).

One example of confirmation for the ministry occurred during another day at work while I listened to my all-time favorite pastor, Steven Furtick. He was speaking on a series called "Surrounded". Pastor Steven told about how the church he planted in Charlotte, North Carolina, was surrounded by Interstate 485.

Chapter 1 - The Genesis

While listening, I got a phone call from a Discover Card customer who lived in a city in North Carolina called Hope Mills. I looked it up on Google Maps because I was interested to see how close she lived to Charlotte so that I could ask her if she knew about Pastor Steven Furtick. After that phone call ended, I received another call moments later from a customer who lived in another city in North Carolina called Sapphire. This city was on the opposite side of town from Hope Mills on the outskirts of Charlotte.

About a year prior to this incident, my wife Cindy and I were about to have a baby girl and when we were thinking of names to call her the Bible verse Jeremiah 29:11 kept coming up: "Plans to give you a hope and a future." Both my wife and I were in total agreement that we should name our new baby girl, Hope. Then as we were deciding on a middle name, we heard a message from one of our pastors, Todd Clark, which blew our minds. It was a message that talked about how heaven is so much greater than earth. He explained about the twelve precious foundational stones in heaven and one of those stones was Sapphire. **"The foundations of the city walls were decorated with every kind of precious stone. The first foundation was jasper, the second sapphire, the third agate, the fourth emerald"** Revelation 21:19 (NIV). So, we chose Sapphire to be our daughter's middle name. When our beautiful daughter was born, Hope Sapphire Wickert became her name.

Now, do those names ring a bell? Hope and Sapphire were the names of those two cities from those two random phone calls I received at work.

Back to Pastor Furtick's message "Surrounded". All of a sudden, he started preaching about a verse in Isaiah chapter forty-eight, specifically verse 5 that says, **"That is why I told you what would happen; I told you beforehand what I was going to**

13

Hope in Numbers

do. Then you could never say, 'My idols did it. My wooden image and metal god commanded it to happen!" Then Pastor Furtick said to his congregation, "Did you see what I did there? The I-485 surrounds this church and there is a promise from God hidden in Isaiah 48:5." Then he waited a moment. "Come on people that took me months to figure out a verse that correlates with the number of the interstate!"

I stopped dead in my tracks. *Whoa, did he just do that?* My favorite pastor of all time was seeing a Bible verse in a number out in the world just like I was. What Pastor Steven had just figured out was that God has posted promises all over the world through numbers. **"I'm single-minded in pursuit of you; don't let me miss the road signs you've posted"** Psalms 119:10 (MSG). I said to myself, *Wow, I have to think of a name to call this idea!*

Later on, as I went on break, I went to my daily prayer spot by a light pole that had the number "15" on it. Every time I would see this sign, it reminded me of a few things. First, it reminded me of Tim Tebow who wears #15 and how he is unashamed of being a man of faith and would take a knee and pray before, during and after his football games. They call what he did "Tebowing" — taking a knee in prayer to the Lord. It also reminded me of the verse in James 1:5 (NIV) which says, **"If any of you lacks wisdom, you should ask God, who gives generously to all without finding fault, and it will be given to you."** So I did exactly what I did pretty much every day. I took a Tim Tebow knee right there outside of my work and I prayed to God and asked for wisdom to come up with a cool name to call this idea.

As I continued on my walk, I was still in awe by those two phone calls that came in earlier that day, one from the city of Hope Mills, North Carolina and another from the city of Sapphire, North Carolina, which are my youngest daughter's first and middle name—Hope Sapphire! Both of these cities surrounded Charlotte, North Carolina where my favorite pastor Steven Furtick preached a message called "Surrounded". Then he quoted a Bible verse in reference to the number from Interstate 485 which surrounds his church!

This was a total answer to prayers because at the time in my life I was praying to God asking Him *Is this idea from you? Is this what you created me to do? Lord Jesus, please show me some signs that this idea is from you, and if it is I'll dedicate my life to this mission of teaching people to see Hope in Numbers.* The sequence of strange events that occurred that day encouraged my soul and it was complete confirmation to me that I wasn't crazy and this idea of seeing God's Word in every number you see actually works, and it will encourage others who love God and the !

As a Christian, I don't believe so much in coincidences as in divine encounters and occurrences. My daughter, Hope, was stuck in my head because of the divine encounter I had that day at work. As I prayed for wisdom, I asked God, "God, please give me something to call this idea. I Hope…" I kept waiting and thinking. *I found hope in these numbers… Hope. In. Numbers. Yes! That's it!* God gave me the name to help other people find hope in numbers!

Also, maybe there can be an acronym for the word HOPE? I thought, *Okay, God help me, is there an acronym for this?* I prayed, and then it came over me as if God had whispered it directly into my ear—**H**olding **O**nto **P**romises **E**verywhere!

Boom! That's it! That's the name of the ministry that's going to change every number into a promise from God! This could literally change the lives of so many people who desire to walk out their faith and be constantly reminded of God's living Word. There was no doubt in my mind that God had revealed the name of this ministry to me. **"I received my message from no human source, and no one taught me. Instead, I received it by direct revelation from Jesus Christ"** Galatians 1:12 (NLT).

Following is a heartfelt testimony of how Hope in Numbers is working in the Life of Pastor Caleb Harrison. Hope in Numbers has helped him carry Jesus with him everywhere he goes.

> *Throughout Scripture we read of many ways that God has spoken to His people throughout the centuries. The Bible tells us that God is at all times holding all things together. In the Great Commission, God gives us the most important command of all, but also the biggest promise. Jesus tells us to go everywhere and make disciples, but that He is with us always. At every waking moment God is with me and among us. Our Father in Heaven is always prompting us to slow down and do life with Him – and to recognize Him speaking to us.*
>
> **"Walk with me and work with me – watch how I do it. Learn the unforced rhythms of grace. I won't lay anything heavy or ill-fitting on you"**
> *Matthew 11:29 (MSG).*
>
> **Hope In Numbers** *does all of this. It has helped me and so many others to hear God speaking. While Jesus is*

walking with us at every moment, the distractions of this world can easily steal our attention and begin to give our enemy a foothold in our lives. **Hope In Numbers** *redirects our attention and turns us back to the truth. Using* **Hope In Numbers** *this past year has brought God's promises back to the center of my life – in traffic, at sporting events, while paying bills, dialing phone numbers, pumping gas, and everyday situations.*

"Let's keep a firm grip on the promises that keep us going. He always keeps his word" Hebrews 10:23 (MSG).

As one of the pastors at our church, I get to see Gordon often and see firsthand the way he leads and disciples others through this work. Most weekends, I get to introduce Gordon to someone new and see how he puts a smile on their face and a little extra hope in their hearts. "Not to impress, but to bless." We are told to always be ready to tell people why we feel blessed, and I've seen that time and time again with Gordon and through using **Hope In Numbers** *myself.*

"But honor the Messiah as Lord in your hearts. Always be ready to give a defense to anyone who asks you for a reason for the hope that is in you"
1 Peter 3:15 (HCSB).

My Noah's Ark

In the very first book of the Bible, in Genesis chapter 6, God gave Noah a great task to build an ark that would save the world and humanity. The world had become so corrupt and sinful without repentance that the justice and sovereignty of God decided to flood the earth, wipeout humanity, and start over with just Noah and his family. When God told Noah his mission to build an ark and save humanity, Noah started building his ark by faith because Noah believed that God was faithful to keep His word.

I believe that I had my own Noah's Ark moment on December 7, 2001, when God gave me a similar mission to fulfill. On this day, I truly felt God tell me, "Gordon, you are going to do something crazy big for Me that will change this world for Jesus." I believed in God, and for over fifteen years of living out this idea and trying it with other people, the Ark of Hope in Numbers is about to set sail, and you are welcome to jump on board!

Looking back, here is the Hope in Numbers for the day I gave my life to Jesus and became a born-again Christian at a conference called "Acquire the Fire". It was on December 7, 2001, which correlates with 1 Corinthians 12:7 (NLT): **"A spiritual gift is given to each of us so we can help each other."** This was the actual day that I received the gift of Hope in Numbers because God knew He was going to develop this spiritual gift from within me from day one. Isn't It amazing how God knows our purpose before we can even walk It out?

I believe God gives his children the task of building an ark or the courage to join someone else's ark project. For example, when people serve at a local church, they help build their senior pastor's ark. Others, on the other hand, are called to make a specific ark that God places in their hearts and ask others to join THEIR project. What is your ark? Who is your team? I thank God for leading me to team with a Christian organization called Joint Venture Creations, which helped me with the phases of building this ark.

Let's get back to the story of Noah. Noah started building this massive ark in the middle of the desert for a flood that no one even believed was coming, except Noah and family. I would be willing to bet that people started criticizing and hating on Noah for building such an enormous ark for no apparent reason other than his faith. I want to forewarn you that the same criticism will happen to you as a Christian who wants to build an ark for God!

I found a great Bible verse to put critics and "haters" into perspective that really helped me bypass them and use them as motivators. A short and easy saying to remember goes like this: "Haters gonna hate. Proverbs 9:8." The actual verse in the Bible says, **"So don't bother correcting mockers; they will only hate you. But correct the wise, and they will love you"** Proverbs 9:8 (NLT). Pastor Steven Furtick stated in a message: "Haters are nothing but validators." I agree that haters can try to invalidate God's will in your life, but you should continue to build your ark for the Lord.

I've had a few haters myself for starting Hope in Numbers, but I take it as a compliment that I'm doing something right because I know that all I am doing is teaching people to see Bible verses out in the real world. Here is what some of my naysayers say about Hope in Numbers. They say, "It seems like you're cherry-picking Bible verses out of context, and when you do that, you can make the verse say whatever you want it to." Trust me when I say this— that's not my heart! Not even for a second! I'm all about reading the Bible in context and knowing the history and intent behind it. I've gone through two years of Bible school and understand the importance of keeping scripture in context. It's easier to memorize a few main verses that show the moral of the story rather than the whole chapter.

I don't want to offend anyone or take anything out of context so for years I've prayed Psalm 139:23-24 to make sure that my heart was on the right track. The psalmist says, **"Search me, O God, and know my heart; test me and know my anxious** thoughts. **Point out anything in me that offends you, and lead me along the path of everlasting life"** Psalm 139:23-24 (NLT).

God reminded me of the story in the book of Matthew in chapters 3 and 4. Here you find Jesus, who is about to start His three-and-a-half-year ministry on earth after being baptized by John the Baptist. After being baptized, Jesus was led into the desert to be tempted by the devil. **"After fasting forty days and forty nights, he was hungry. The tempter came to him and said, 'If you are the Son of God, tell these stones to become bread'"** Matthew 4:2-3 (NIV). Let's stop right here. Temptation came to Jesus. The devil tried to transition the mind and thoughts of Jesus from the spiritual cleanse in fasting to the fleshly desires of eating. The devil will always go after our thoughts to tamper with them. So, we must do as Jesus did and keep our thoughts firmly planted on God's truths and promises.

Here is what Jesus did next: **"Jesus answered, 'It is written: 'Man shall not live on bread alone, but on every word that comes from the mouth of God'"** Matthew 4:4 (NIV). Did you notice what Jesus did? He quoted scripture from memory to defeat the temptation. Specifically, he quoted scripture about how powerful the Word of God is to keep us alive and well. Jesus beautifully stated and demonstrated how we are not able to live on just physical food but on every word that comes from God. Hope in Numbers can help us live on every word that comes from God.

Let's continue. **"Then the devil took him to the holy city and had him stand on the highest point of the temple. 'If you are the Son of God,' he said, 'throw yourself down. For it is written: 'He will command his angels concerning you, and they will lift you up in their hands, so that you will not strike your foot against a stone'"** Matthew 4:5-6 (NIV). Now, the devil was trying to use God's Word to convince Jesus to put himself in harm's way, but Jesus knew the devil was twisting God's Word. He knew the truth because He knew scripture. Jesus was the Word that became flesh and could confidently reply with this: **"It is also written: 'Do not put the Lord your God to the test'"** Matthew 4:7 (NIV). Again, Jesus memorized scripture and used it when he was at a moment when it counted the most. This concept can work for you too! You can use scripture to defeat the devil by knowing the truths that will disarm his attacks!

Let's keep continue. Here's what happened next. **"Again, the devil took him to a very high mountain and showed him all the kingdoms of the world and their splendor. "All this I will give you," he said, "if you will bow down and worship me." Jesus said to him, "Away from me, Satan! For it is written: 'Worship the Lord your God, and serve him only." Then the devil left him, and angels came and attended him"** Matthew 4:1-11 (NIV). Wow! Did you notice what happened here? Jesus defeated every temptation with a scripture from God that made the devil flee from Him! The devil did not bother to stick around and try to deceive Jesus any longer. The devil likely went off to find somebody else who did not hold onto the Word of God so firmly.

We can be like Jesus in this way: by being a person of strong faith, who knows the truth, memorizes scripture, and uses its devil destroying power when temptations and trials come our way!. **"The temptations in your life are no different from what others experience. And God is faithful. He will not allow the temptation to be more than you can stand. When you are tempted, he will show you a way out so that you can endure"** 1 Corinthians 10:13 (NLT).

I believe seeing Hope in Numbers will do what that verse above says. I can't count how many times I've used Hope in Numbers during tempting situations to destroy the temptation right on the spot. Boom! Gone in a second because the numbers reminded me of powerful sin-killing truths found in God's Word. Seeing Hope in Numbers helps demolish strongholds like addiction, fear, doubt, anger, lust, and other sin you haven't been able to wish away on your own.

The Six Most Frequently Asked Questions

I've spent many years memorizing Bible verses and practicing this gift. I have instilled close to one thousand Bible verses to memory, but don't let that discourage you from trying it yourself! Please know this—everybody starts with ZERO Bible verses memorized! "Do not despise these small beginnings, for the Lord rejoices to see the work begin" Zechariah 4:10 (NLT). So, to help you get passed some initial questions or concerns, here are six of the most Frequently Asked Questions about Hope in Numbers with answers and a plan of action for you to begin your Hope in Numbers journey!

WHO is Hope in Numbers for? I believe Hope in Numbers is for anyone who truly desires to try this and who loves God's Word. I've seen it many times first hand with my friends and family who do this and it blesses their lives. They tell me their Hope in Numbers stories and I get overwhelmed with joy when they tell me how it's changing their day to day life. Henry Ford once said, "Whether you think you can or whether you think you can't, you're right." So if you truly believe you can do this, you are right, you can do it! The other way reigns true as well. If you don't believe you can, you are also right. Sure, doubts may rise up when you start trying this at first, but if you truly want to do this you need to doubt your doubts because they are as empty as the tomb Jesus walked out of! You CAN do this!

WHAT verses should I start memorizing? Start with verses that you already know or like, then memorize and connect the number to the verse. So, take inventory of what verses you may already know by heart, find out the number verse it is, and start to train your mind so that whenever you see that number, you either say the verse out loud or quietly rehearse it in your head.

WHERE do I find Hope in Numbers? The answer to this question is, everywhere! Literally, everywhere you go there will be numbers. A few examples of places where I find Hope in Numbers are license plates, speed limit signs, home addresses, phone numbers, time of day, date, locker combo, jerseys, dart boards, pool table balls, receipts, treadmills, and the list goes on and on! Hope can be found in classrooms, in the streets, at work, in church, at sports games, and much more! This makes living the Word and memorizing Bible verses very exciting as a Christian.

WHEN can I practice Hope in Numbers? Some people will say that they do not have time to read the Bible or memorize scriptures. That simply is not true. Louie Giglio once said, "You always have time for the things you do first." I totally agree. If you truly desire to do something, you can always make time for it by either waking up earlier or doing it first thing once you wake up.

HOW do I start to see Hope in Numbers? Just pray to receive the gift of seeing Hope in Numbers. Ask God to open your eyes to see and be reminded of His promises. You can pray this Psalm, which correlates with the book's publication date of January 19, 2018. **"Open my eyes to see the wonderful truths in your instructions"** Psalm 119:18 (NLT). Anything is possible with God, and when you ask Him in sincere prayer that you would like to receive this gift, I believe He will give you the strength and vision to begin this journey. **"Ask and it will be given to you; seek and you will find; knock and the door will be opened to you"** Matthew 7:7 (NIV).

WHY should I want to see Hope in Numbers? My answer to this question is simple—to be truly blessed! The Bible is sixty-six love letters from God written to us to know Him more intimately. Our Heavenly Father places His mysteries in these books so He can reveal himself to those who believe. Satan is a con artist full of lies and deception, which he tries to get us to believe and act on daily. Hope in Numbers continually fills us with God's Holy Word so that there is no room left for Satan's lies. **"Who will win the battle against the world? Only those who believe that Jesus Christ is the Son of God"** 1 John 5:5 (NLT). Yes, this is how you win the battle against the world!

Hope in Numbers has the power to defeat temptations, encourage righteous living, and create an unexplainable sense of peace in all circumstances, good or bad. It will cause you to live boldly and proclaim your faith confidently to others . Hope in Numbers can do these things and more because we are simply using God's Word as our weapon! **"For the word of God is alive and active. Sharper than any double-edged sword, it penetrates even to dividing soul and spirit, joints and marrow; it judges the thoughts and attitudes of the heart"** Hebrews 4:12 (NIV). We will win the battle against the world because we are using God's Word as our defender. **"He will cover you with his feathers. He will shelter you with his wings. His faithful promises are your armor and protection"** Psalm 91:4 (NLT).

This book brakes down into five simple steps for you. These are your keys for holding onto these promises from God and seeing them out in the world. Just like the cover of this book has a handprint with all five fingers holding onto the book, you also must use all five of these steps to hold onto promises everywhere. The five steps are outlined for you using the word TRUTH as an acronym to make it easier for you to remember and apply.

Here are the five steps:

T ry it
R enew it
U se it
T each it
H old it

In the following five chapters, I will go deeper into how to accomplish each step and give you a clearer understanding of how you can start seeing Hope in Numbers for yourself starting today! This can and will change how you see the world forever. I can't wait for this gift to come to fruition in your life and be a huge blessing for you and your family!

CHAPTER 2 - TRY IT

One thing I loved when growing up was going to Costco supermarket stores and just walking around and sampling free foods and drinks. I would go to a bunch of the sample stations with food and drinks and try them all! It's a genius marketing strategy because these companies knew if potential customers tasted and saw how good their products were. Then they might become customers for life. If they become customers for life, they would likely tell their friends and family about the product.

The same goes with God's Word and seeing Hope in Numbers! **"Taste and see that the Lord is good. Oh, the joys of those who take refuge in him!"** Psalm 34:8 (NLT). My promise to you is that once you taste and see how good the Lord is by consuming His Word every day, then you will be a consumer of God's Word for life! Remember, Jesus is the bread of life, and there is no doubt you will love His Word that nourishes you and provides for your every need!

You've probably already tried Hope in Numbers when you looked up your Birthday Bible verse in the back! Do that now if you haven't. Your birth date is just the beginning! Do you have any other special dates that come to mind in your life? Any anniversary, graduation, family members' birthdays, and even today's date has a significant promise. Go and taste and see how good our God is with your special dates!

Attitude is Key
A quick story explains the key to unlocking God's promises in numbers —attitude. Our attitude towards this new practice will determine if we succeed at seeing God's Word everywhere we go or not. If you understand the power of attitude, you will have an advantage over others who do not understand. **"Be made new in the attitude of your minds"** Ephesians 4:23 (NIV).

After a victory over Baylor in the 2017 NCAA March Madness Tournament game, South Carolina Head Coach Frank Martin was asked a great question by Max, a young reporter from Sports Illustrated Kids. Max asked, "When you coach and teach your team defense, what's more important, technique or attitude?" Coach Martin answered, "First of all, a lot of respect to you. That's a heck of a question. I've been doing this a long time, and that's the first time anyone's ever asked me that, that's a heck of the question." Then Coach Martin answered, "Attitude comes first. We gotta have guys that are gonna believe in our mission, that are going to believe in what we do. Once they believe, then we can teach them the techniques. It all starts with our mindset; we have guys that are completely bought into.

Did you catch that? This successful college coach said you must believe in what you are doing before learning how to do it. Do you believe that holding onto promises everywhere will benefit every aspect of your life? Do you believe your perspective will radically transform by renewing your mind in God's Word daily? If you believe in the significance of this practice and understand the mission, then you are on the right path to discover the significant value of the rest of this book.

In reality, this book is like the seed in the parable of the sower. Some people will act like the seed that fell on the path and won't be receptive to this gift. Others will be like the soil that is too rocky, and the roots won't be able to grow deep enough to sustain this new practice. Others will be like the soil surrounded by thorns and appreciate the idea but will likely go back to seeing the world as other people see it- not fully discovering how to find God in it.

I truly hope you will be like the good soil that produces a crop one hundred, sixty, and thirty-fold of that which was sown! Hope in Numbers can produce a crop of blessings and favor that can forever bless your life and the lives of those whom you touch. It all starts with your heart and attitude towards God's Word.

Open Heart Surgery

I was born on September 21, 1981, and from day one, my parents knew I needed open heart surgery around fifteen years old. When I was born, the ultrasounds showed that I had a dysfunctional heart and would need parts of my heart replaced when the doctors thought my heart reached full size. The issue was that my aortic valve wasn't open fully. If my heart rate got up too high, I could likely die.

So, growing up, running long distances, and playing sports correctly - with complete effort, was prohibited! I was blessed with natural athleticism with a dream to become a professional baseball player, so this was difficult for me. Honestly, I couldn't wait to have open heart surgery so I could start really running around and playing sports.

Near the end of my freshman year of high school in 1996, my parents and the doctors decided it was time to replace my aortic valve. My open-heart surgery was scheduled for May 7, 1996. I remember the night before my surgery like it was yesterday. My brothers and I wanted to act out what the doctors were going to do to me on the operation table, so I laid down on my bed while my brothers got a knife and pretended to cut open my chest and replace my valve. I know, crazy kids, right? I was just extremely excited to get a properly working heart so I could live my life and be active.

Honestly, I wasn't nervous or fearful at all about the surgery. I'm not sure why, but I felt a sense of peace about moving forward. **"My flesh and my heart may fail, but God is the strength of my heart and my portion forever"** Psalm 73:26 (NIV). I now know that Jesus was watching over me and protecting me during that time. The surgery I underwent was called The Ross Procedure. I remember searching the internet for the exact details. I had the same open-heart surgery that Arnold Schwarzenegger and at around the same age. I thought that was so cool back then. I mean, if the TERMINATOR can do it, so can I!

The surgery happened, and everything went according to plan. I was in the hospital for about six days before going home. They gave me strict instructions not to lift anything heavy or do any strenuous activity involving heavy breathing for six months. However, I was young, reckless, feeling amazing after the surgery. So, within a week of getting out of the hospital, I was doing flips off our diving board to impress a girl I liked. This was a big no-no from the doctors, but I couldn't help myself because I felt like I had a new start in life.

Chapter 2 - Try it

Shortly after recklessly flipping off the diving board, I had another occurrence that caused a lot of strain on my chest. When I was at Peter Piper Pizza one day with my friends, I decided to unscrew the lid to a crushed red pepper shaker on our table so the next person to grab the pepper shaker would dump the pepper all over their pizza. I'm a jokester, and I thought it would be funny to see their reaction. Unfortunately, the girl who picked up the red pepper did not find it funny at all! She grabbed some of the peppers and threw them in my face. I jumped back and panicked in pain because some of the red peppers got stuck in my eyes! I jumped around, punched walls, and screamed in pain. Not something my doctors would have been happy to see just a week or two after my open-heart surgery.

Within the same week, a third very obnoxious event happened. One of our neighbors at the time came over to our house under the influence of alcohol. He was really drunk and was yelling and cussing at my mother while my dad was out of town. I was the only son at home and wouldn't let this drunken guy yell at or be around my mother. So, I had to forcefully get him to leave our house and then slam the door shut!

After all these occurrences, we noticed that I started to get really sick. None of the doctors knew what was happening, but my symptoms were getting worse and worse. Then a young doctor came in to check on me. He listened to my heart and heard something strange undetected by the other doctors.

I was rushed to the ER to have emergency surgery right away because there was a lot of fluid crushing my heart. For weeks I had a chest tube to drain all the excess fluid. That tube saved my life. My family later told me that I literally almost died several times. I know without a doubt that Jesus kept me alive during my heart dysfunction because He was not finished with me yet. **Being confident of this, that he who began a**

good work in you will carry it on to completion until the day of Christ Jesus" Philippians 1:6 (NIV). Out of my mess, there comes a message. Like my dysfunctional heart that needed replacing so I could live, I believe most people's hearts need to be changed and opened to receive more of God's Word. **"Therefore, change your hearts and stop being stubborn"** Deuteronomy 10:16 (NLT). Instead of being vaguely open to this idea of seeing Hope in Numbers, I believe God wants you to be fully open and responsive to receiving this idea and try to see Hope in Numbers so that it can help save your spiritual life from despair!

I do not believe it is a coincidence that you are reading this book. I believe God wants to use you to be a light of the world, and He can only do that if you allow Him to change your heart. **"And I will give you a new heart, and I will put a new spirit in you. I will take out your stony, stubborn heart and give you a tender, responsive heart"** Ezekiel 36:26 (NLT). I could have been bitter about not being born with a healthy heart, but instead it made me better because I appreciate the gift of life and carry with me tremendous joy.

Falling in Love with God's Word

Many of us own a Bible, attend church regularly, and even pray daily, but how many of us truly love God's Word and want to spend precious time with it?

In an account in the gospels, someone came up to Jesus and asked Him, **"'Teacher, which is the great commandment in the Law?' And he said to him, 'You shall love the Lord your God with all your heart and with all your soul and with all your mind'"** Matthew 22:36-37 (ESV). How are we supposed to do that? Well, when you know the significance of what God did for us by sending His son to die for our sins, it becomes a lot easier to love Him! **"For God so loved the world that he gave his one**

and only Son, that whoever believes in him shall not perish but have eternal life" John 3:16 (NIV). When you love God, you want to hear from Him all the time and be in His presence. That is the reason the Bible was written for us—so we can fall deeper in love with God! Hope in Numbers will be impossible for you if you do not love the Word of God because you must want to be around it and see it everywhere for it to work. If you just occasionally dabble in it or know just a little bit about it, it will not last very long.

Falling in love with God's Word is the key! It's very similar to how a man and a woman fall in love. The relationship first starts by being acquaintances with each other. You notice them and begin to talk and interact. Then you start to spend more time together, making memories, and eventually decide to spend the rest of your life together by getting married. Why? Well, because you have fallen in love with each other, and you do not want to live your life without that person. The same concept is necessary with you and God through His Word. You open up the Bible and spend time reading it. Then you begin to make memories with certain verses which speak to you, and when you are finally ready, you decide to be a follower of Christ until you die. Basically, you marry God and His Word. The great news is God already loves you, no matter your sin! **"But God demonstrates his own love for us in this: While we were still sinners, Christ died for us"** Romans 5:8 (NIV). He is simply waiting for you to fall in love with Him!

I'm no marriage expert—you can ask my wife, Cindy—but I can offer you some practical advice if you are having difficulty falling in love with God's Word. You might even think the Bible is boring or confusing, but I am here to help you, and I believe you will start to see how beautifully inspired and transformational the Bible can be! Are you ready?

Hope in Numbers

Here is one piece of advice for those new to the Bible or reading it consistently: Find yourself a coach or a pastor who can help you understand the complexities of God's Word. Think about it this way. In most good movies, the hero always needs a guide or a coach to help them get to where they want to be. Examples include Luke Skywalker needing Yoda in Star Wars, the Karate Kid needing Mr. Miyagi to learn and develop the discipline he needed to succeed, or Lightning McQueen needing the Hudson Hornet to help him win the Piston Cup.

There is an endless list of heroes instructed by someone with a greater understanding and experience than them. The same goes for our own spiritual walks and journeys to understanding and living out God's Word. That is why we need pastors who we resonate with and can understand their teachings clearly.

Falling in love with God's Word is not always an overnight occurrence. Sometimes, it takes longer to fall in love with His Word and make a lifelong commitment to it. Once you do, get ready to experience a life radically transformed by His love, grace, and mercy! His Word will be with you forever to guide you, nourish you, and prosper you. Fall in love with God's Word and see how God will change your life.

How Hope in Numbers Changes Everything

Most people have a daily routine they follow they set their alarm clock for 6:30 am to get up, get ready, and get where they need to be. The ordinary guy wakes up to the sound of his alarm despite his tiredness, gets out of bed, showers, gets dressed, and maybe eats a quick breakfast and is out the door. He pulls out of the driveway onto the road and then meets traffic: brake lights, traffic congestions, red lights, and maybe even someone cuts him off to start his morning, which adds to the frustration of the commute.

Here is how Hope in Numbers changes everything and can change a lethargic life to a life of guidance and strength from God! Let's say, instead of setting your alarm for 6:30 in the morning, you set your alarm to 6:33 a.m. Now, watch this. Once that alarm hits, instead of dreading your day, and wishing to stay in bed longer, you wake up with fire and purpose because you are given a reminder of God's promise in Matthew 6:33 (NIV): **"But seek first his kingdom and his righteousness, and all these things will be given to you as well."**

After getting dressed, you mix yourself a bowl of instant oatmeal, pop it in the microwave, and set the cook time to one minute and sixteen seconds, which triggers you to meditate on Romans 1:16 (NIV) **"For I am not ashamed of the gospel, because it is the power of God that brings salvation to everyone who believes: first to the Jew, then to the Gentile."** Boom.

After breakfast, you get into your car, pull out of the driveway, and see your home address: 2517, which reminds you of 2 Corinthians 5:17 (ESV) **"Therefore, if anyone is in Christ, he is a new creation. The old has passed away; behold, the new has come."** Within the first few precious moments of your day, you have already been refreshed with God's Word three times, and you didn't even need to open up your Bible. With Hope in Numbers, God's Word will be with you always! **"This is the new covenant I will make with my people on that day, says the Lord: I will put my laws in their hearts, and I will write them on their minds"** Hebrews 10:16 (NLT).

As you drive to work or school and traffic hits, you are no longer bothered by the mania of brake lights, red lights, and people that cut in front of you. In fact, you might welcome somebody to pull in front of you so that you can see if they have some Hope in Numbers on their license plates. Imagine that. Here is the beauty of Hope in Numbers: Let's say somebody cuts you off and it stirs up a little anger inside you. Then you notice that the license plate has a 151 in it, which reminds you of Proverbs 15:1 (NIV): **"A gentle answer turns away wrath, but a harsh word stirs up anger."** Just the timely truth that you needed to hear at that moment. Trust me when I say this happens to me all day long!

No longer are the things of this world burdens and distractions. They are blessings and guidance if you wish to see them. Hitting a red light is no longer a waste of time, but an opportunity to be still, seek and find wisdom from God by unlocking Bible verses in the license plates and street signs all around you. **"Be still, and know that I am God!"** Psalm 46:10 (NLT). To be completely honest, I love when I hit a red light because I get to slow down, look around and find God's amazing promises that refuel my soul. It's like a treasure hunt for blessings!

Also, I love to have short Bible studies with my kids in the morning with Hope in Numbers while driving them to school. We find random verses in numbers and talk about their meanings before I drop them off at school. For example, when we see a 35 mile per hour speed limit sign, we talk about Proverbs 3:5 (NIV): **"Trust in the Lord with all your heart and lean not on your own understanding."** I once heard one of my pastors, Todd Clark, say, "The first ten minutes of your day is the rudder of the day." So, I make it my intention to start my kids off in the right direction by talking about the Word of God before school. You can do this with your kids too.

Make this a part of your daily routine because just like we need to wake up our physical body and get dressed every morning, we also need to wake up our soul and put on the full armor of God every morning. A great way to do this is to start your mornings with Hope in Numbers. **"Put on the full armor of God, so that you can take your stand against the devil's schemes"** Ephesians 6:11 (NIV).

Chapter 2 - Try it

Hope in Numbers at the Workplace

As you already know, I discovered Hope in Numbers while at work at Discover Card. I still use Hope in Numbers every day at work. Here's how. Daily I set my break and lunch times to times that remind me of key verses. I have my first break at 8:31 a.m., which matches with Romans 8:31 (NIV): **"If God is for us, who can be against us?"** This is one of my favorite promises from God in the entire Bible. Whenever I feel discouraged or like the world is against me, I meditate on this promise, and it fires me up with great confidence in the Lord.

I would encourage you to do the same. Start taking your breaks at times that remind you of a promise from God in the Bible. For example, you could take an early lunch break at 10:45 a.m. to remind you of Mark 10:45 (NIV): **"For even the Son of Man did not come to be served, but to serve, and to give His life as a ransom for many."** This scripture could remind you of the goodness of God and give you the challenge to be a servant during your lunch break. One scripture can put you in such a grateful state of mind before eating lunch with your co-workers. Try it out!

Another great promise to be reminded of would be from Luke 12:31 (NLT): **"Seek the Kingdom of God above all else, and he will give you everything you need."** Using the time of day for Hope in Numbers at work can and will encourage you to live out your faith! The Word of God has the power to defeat feelings of fear, guilt, shame, depression, and anger. With God's Word constantly flowing through your mind, you will be refreshed with a joyful spirit that will spring up like a spring of water within you. Like Jesus said, **"but whoever drinks the water I give them will never thirst. Indeed, the water I give them will become in them a spring of water welling up to eternal life"** John 4:14 (NIV).

Hope in Numbers

Hope in Numbers at Church*** cover later

Indeed, at church, every week, your pastor preaches the Word of God and teaches you more and more about Jesus and the Kingdom of God. Want to know how to add even more fire to the service? Here's how Hope in Numbers can give your church service and Bible study even more impact! Every church service has a start time and usually an end time. Some church services might start at 8:00 a.m. on Sunday mornings. The church, or you and your family could do, is change that time from 8:00 a.m. to 8:01 a.m. so that the time of the service can remind someone of Romans 8:1 (NIV) **"Therefore, there is now no condemnation for those who are in Christ Jesus."** Now even the time of the service adds life-saving power to your life!

Or you can do this for your own at-home Bible studies. Luke 6:31(NIV) is a good time to start studies: **"Do to others as you would have them do to you."** Now the entire Bible study can be centered around the golden rule. It will be easier to implement this scripture when you dedicate the start time of the Bible study to it! Give it a try! If you have a church service or Bible study starting at 8:30 a.m., let others know that it begins at 8:31 because Romans 8:31 (NIV) says, **"If God is for us, who can be against us?"** Who wouldn't want to be reminded of that significant promise right before worshiping the Lord?

Also, you can turn all the room numbers of the church buildings into promises. When I walk up to Christ's Church of the Valley, I see a huge "3 yrs - 6 yrs" sign on a building. Proverbs 3:6 (NIV) says, **"In all your ways submit to him, and he will make your paths straight."** The sign on the high school building says "7th -12th Grade", which can become Matthew 7:12 (NIV) with Hope in Numbers: **"So in everything, do to others what you would have them do to you, for this sums up the Law and the Prophets."** Find some of your Hope in Numbers around your church and get blessed by His Word!

Chapter 2 - Try it

Hope in Numbers at School

One of the goals of the Hope in Numbers ministry is to bring God's Word back into workplaces and especially classrooms around the world. In a world where school systems are turning away from God, Hope in Numbers is on a mission to infiltrate workplaces and schools with the Word of God so that salvation can reign! Here's one way we can infiltrate the classrooms with the Word of God: Let's say you or your child gets a bad grade on a homework assignment or a test, say sixty-nine percent (a D). A poor score, according to the grading system. Instead of feeling discouraged and giving up, you are reminded of Galatians 6:9 (NLT), which says, **"So let's not get tired of doing what is good. At just the right time, we will reap a harvest of blessing if we don't give up."** You can write out this verse next to your grade on the assignment and meditate on God's promise, feeling loved and encouraged, instead of feeling devastated about one poor score.

Here is another example. Sometimes math class can be extremely confusing at times causing feelings of anxiety to rise. Your teacher turns to write on the chalkboard '1433' for the solution of a math equation. Most students will not notice the power and encouragement here, but you will since you are a student of Hope in Numbers! The solution 1433 can remind you of a real solution found in 1 Corinthians 14:33a (ESV), **"For God is not a God of confusion but of peace."** This promise would warm your heart with comfort, knowing that God will provide you with peace because God is a good, good Father. Can I get an amen?

Most high schools have lockers for every student. Hope in Numbers works great on locker numbers! Imagine getting a locker that encourages you every day of your high school career! That is exactly what Hope in Numbers can do for high school students. For example, if your locker number was 119, you could be reminded daily of 1 Timothy 1:19 (NLT) which teaches, **"Cling to your faith in Christ, and keep your conscience clear. For some people have deliberately violated their consciences; as a result, their faith has been shipwrecked."** How blessed would you be to be reminded daily by Hope in Numbers to live out these promises while in high school?

Hear a testimony from a high school student from my youth group whom I teach Hope in Numbers to. His name is Luke:

> *One morning, after waking up early for yet another school day, my guard was down, and I was not focused on the truth. The first time I can remember putting Hope In Numbers into use was on a regular morning at school. Day after day, and class after class, the strong foundation God provides is easy to forget when I don't start my day with the Word. Sitting in math class, I put down my answer for a question of my homework, soon realizing it also had my favorite verse in it. My answer of 163 transformed into Proverbs 16:3: "Commit to the Lord whatever you do, and he will establish your plans." Suddenly I'm reminded I need to treat the school day with importance and give it my all, whilst representing a great attitude in representation of my faith.*
>
> *A foundation built on rock never trembles. In contrast, a foundation built upon sand will crumble. The streams may rise, and the winds will rage, yet the house strengthened by rock will never fall. Hope in Numbers has taught me how to put my faith in use every day, and for me. It has been the strong foundation that keeps Jesus in control. As a junior in high school, distractions are*

everywhere, but so are numbers. From waking up early in the morning and looking at the alarm clock, to math class, you can find verses that help encourage you to take control of your day in the name of Christ. Gordon has mentored me and many others to show us how to take those numbers back, turning one number into one verse, and changing one life forever.

God's Word is strength when we are weak because God is our defender. Engraving encouraging verses into the mind and putting them into use will reveal exactly this. Becoming a man in Christ is something that I can always work on and remembering Bible verses furthers the strong foundation in the pursuit to achieve this. Hope in Numbers fights the battles we can't see. Put it into use and the Word of God will shine with perfect clarity.

With Hope,
Luke Unverferth

Luke isa great example of a young leader fighting the good fight of faith at his school! **"Let us not become weary in doing good, for at the proper time we will reap a harvest if we do not give up"** Galatians 6:9 (NIV).

We can be ambassadors for Him by using this gift of seeing and reciting Bible verses everywhere we go! Let us live out our faith by being strong and courageous for others. What can be better than sharing your faith with somebody and witnessing them get saved? That is why knowing Hope in Numbers and practicing it at work or school has such power because we have the potential to witness boldly to others. We, as Christians, are some of the only "Bibles" people will ever read! Through our words, our actions, and our character, people can start to see and know Christ through us! **"Therefore, since we are surrounded by such a great cloud of witnesses, let us throw off everything that hinders and the sin that so easily entangles. And let us run with perseverance the race marked out for us"** Hebrews 12:1 (NIV).

Hope in Numbers in Sports

Another great arena to bring God's Word back into the secular world is through sports. Sports are universally popular pastime with a tremendous ability to influence and reach people. I used to watch a lot of sports before I was on fire for the Lord. I would geek out about the statistics of many star players in each sport. Once I started Hope in Numbers, my passion for God's word far surpassed that of sports. **"I once thought these things were valuable, but now I consider them worthless because of what Christ has done. Yes, everything else is worthless when compared with the infinite value of knowing Christ Jesus my Lord. For his sake, I have discarded everything else, counting it all as garbage, so that I could gain Christ"** Philippians 3:7-8 (NLT). I now see God's Word in every sports game and in every jersey number. It is simply life-changing what Hope in Numbers can do.

Hope in Numbers is great for those still active in sports. Here are some examples of how you can be reminded of God's Truth while playing on a sports team. Let's say you see jersey number 24 on the field or court and realize you have been playing selfishly. With Hope in Numbers, you remember Philippians 2:4 (NLT): **"Don't look out only for your own interests, but take an interest in others, too."** It is neat experiencing the power of Hope in Numbers on a field, court, or in the stands at a sports event. In one moment, you are self-centered and focused on your concerns, and then the next, God hits you with a powerful Truth that can flip your entire attitude toward His Kingdom.

Let's say that your baseball game starts at 3:30 p.m. today, and you want to focus on Jesus shining through you during the game. Hope in Numbers for that time is: **"He must become greater and greater, and I must become less and less"** John 3:30 (NLT). Then let's say you are stressing out in the bottom of the 9th inning because it's a tied game with the winning run on third base, and the count is 3-balls and 2-strikes. The score reminds you of Colossians 3:2 (NIV), and your anxiety is relieved because God's Word reminds you to **"set your minds on things above, not on earthly things."** Are you seeing how all this applies to almost any situation?

Now let's try this for the game of football. Let's say a team gets a first down, and it is 1st and 10, which can now remind you of Galatians 1:10 (NLT) **"Obviously, I'm not trying to win the approval of people, but of God. If pleasing people were my goal, I would not be Christ's servant."** This verse can bring you back into the right perspective instantly of your true mission and calling in life.

Another play happens, and the defensive lineman gets called for roughing the passer and gets charged a 15-yard penalty. You could get mad, or you could be reminded of James 1:5 (NIV), **"If any of you lacks wisdom, you should ask God, who gives generously to all without finding fault, and it will be given to you."** Now that is growing in your spiritual walk during a game! Don't get mad; ask God for wisdom!

Finally, for those Patriot fans out there, let's say you are watching a game, and you are fearful because the team you are up against is having an exceptional season. You see Tom Brady's jersey with the number twelve, which reminds you of James 1:2 (NIV) **"Consider it pure joy, my brothers and sisters, whenever you face trials of many kinds."** Now you can go out there with a new sense of confidence and joy in your heart for facing such a difficult task!

Take Baby Steps

When a baby is born into this world, the baby knows very few things other than how to eat, sleep, cry and fill up diapers. The baby does not yet know how to walk, talk, read, and definitely does not know how to memorize Bible verses! Yet, the baby is curious and is willing to try new things. When the baby sees somebody who can walk, the baby builds up the desire to try walking. The baby tries to get up on two feet and inevitably falls, but the baby doesn't stop there. The baby gets up and tries it again and again until it finally happens; the baby has learned how to walk! The baby gets so good at walking that it becomes second nature, and they no longer must think about it.

Replication of others' behavior repeatedly happens in our lives. We see something that others have done or are doing successfully, and we build up curiosity and the desire to do it too. My job is to make you curious and build up the desire in your heart to want to do Hope and Numbers yourself! Once you try and decide not to give up, your life will never be the same! Blessings will be with you everywhere you go!

Hear a personal testimony from a professional baseball player that I met named James Jones, and how simply trying Hope in Numbers has changed is faith journey:

> *You will never meet someone like Gordon Wickert. After being introduced to him at a CCV student ministry service, I knew there was something special with him. Gordon opened the eyes of my heart, of what it is like to cherish God's Word. I wanted to get straight into the Word when he was connecting a verse to every number that came across in our conversation. My birthday, my wife's birthday, my Jersey number, my phone number—it was absolutely mind-blowing listening and witnessing his love for the Word. To be*

honest, I was quite intimidated thinking about how I could get to the point of storing God's Word in my heart, but Gordon's encouragement was what I needed. He simply said, "Try it" and that's exactly what I did. By starting with one verse and expectantly looking for it, my relationship with God became more intimate. The verses were everywhere. Some were in obvious places and some in not so obvious places. This made me feel God's presence wherever my day took me. I felt like God was leaving His fingerprints everywhere. Practicing Hope in Numbers brought a revelation of Deuteronomy 31:6: "Be strong and courageous. Do not fear or be in dread of them, for it is the LORD your God who goes with you. He will not leave you or forsake you." This book will be a huge blessing to your life if you would simply make a decision try it!

James Jones

-Pitcher in Texas Rangers organization

Take James' advice. Even if it is a small step, or an easy verse, just simply start. You won't regret it!

You Are Either Growing or Dying

I have learned from personal experience that the most frustrating and difficult times in life come when I am not growing, learning, or getting closer to God. I love to learn and hear more about Jesus, the stories in the Bible, new worship songs, and meet new people. Yet, I feel at my worst when I'm not pursuing something new or acquiring a new Bible verse. When I am stuck like this, the devil has an opportunity to win the battle for Hope that day. That's why I like to tell people to be a moving target for Jesus so that the devil can't hit them with his arrows. Keep moving forward no matter what! **"The righteous keep moving forward, and those with clean hands become stronger and stronger"** Job 17:9 (NLT).

You may have experienced being in a spot where you feel bored and stuck because you are not growing physically, mentally, or spiritually. You experience those emotions because God put in your DNA a desire for consistent growth. Jesus came to give us an abundant life, not a stagnant one. **"I came that they may have life, and have it abundantly"** John 10:10b (ESV). We must continue to press forward and grow in Christ by learning more about Him daily.

The act of trying something new initiates the growth process. If we decide not to try something new, growth will never happen. The truth of the matter is: if you are not growing, then you're simply dying. The possibilities and the doors that open become endless when we try something new. Look back and see how the act of speaking a language, writing, and creating technology, have opened doors of opportunities for human civilization. When you dare to try something new, you add so much to the quality of life.

Since we have the desire and ability to grow physically, mentally, and spiritually, let us choose to do so. Not everybody gets that chance. Not everybody gets that opportunity to freely learn, read, and grow. I know someone very special and close to my heart who was not given that chance. I want to introduce you to my son, Andrew.

My Son Andrew

In 2008, my first wife and I received some of the best news in the world. We were going to have a baby! We already had a daughter together named Emily Grace, so adding a new addition to the family was going to be amazing! We couldn't wait for the twenty-week appointment to find out the gender of the baby. We were so excited and had baby names already picked out.

Chapter 2 - Try it

We arrived at the appointment, and the ultrasound tech spent over one hour showing us every part of the baby's body. The tech said, "Look at his legs. He's going to be a runner!" Did I hear her right? She said that the baby was a he! This was a dream come true for me. The tech told us we were having a baby boy. I always wanted a boy to teach him all the sports and how to be a godly man! I had the name Nash picked out after Steve Nash from the Phoenix Suns, one of my favorite basketball players. At work, on the first ultrasound picture we got months before, I actually put the head of Steve Nash on the little peanut. I dreamed of him being in the NBA one day. We were so excited!

Then moments later, the joy in the room vanished. Our whole world got turned upside down. The attitude of the ultrasound tech abruptly changed when she moved the ultrasound toward the baby's head. It started to scare us, but she couldn't tell us anything. She left the room immediately to go and get the doctor. They moved us to a different room, and we waited anxiously to find out what was happening.

What happened next shook us to the core of our faith and trust in God. The doctor walked in to break the bad news to us. "Parents, your baby boy has no brain at all. We see only water inside of his head." The knot in my stomach was indescribable. We started crying uncontrollably. Then I asked, "Is there any chance for him to live?" The doctor said, "No, he has a zero percent chance of survival." I was in disbelief. "Zero percent?" I kept asking as tears fell down my face uncontrollably

Andrew's condition was called Hydrocephalus - hydro stands for water, and Cephalus meaning brain. Basically, in layman's terms, water crushed his brain, and there was no sign of his brain. The doctors told us we should abort him, which goes against my faith. He then asked us if we wanted to take a test to find out what caused this condition. We agreed so we could find

Hope in Numbers

out what caused this, because it would help to know if we could have more kids or not. The test occurred right then and there in the doctor's office. The doctor stuck a large needle into the womb to get fluid to test it. The doctor told us that in doing the test, we had a 1/150 chance of losing the baby right then and there. We did the test, and it went smoothly, thank God!

We were heartbroken, frightened, and needed wisdom fast, so we ran to our church for support. Pastors and friends rushed over to pray with us for a miracle of healing. I didn't know this at the time but looking back at the Hope in Numbers for that day, when we found out this horrible news, it was so encouraging to know that Jesus was with us the entire time. 5/7 was the date we found out about Andrew's condition, and 1 Peter 5:7 says, **"Cast all your anxiety on him because he cares for you."** That's exactly what we did. We asked God to show up in a huge way. We also asked everyone we knew to pray for a miracle for our baby boy.

The next five days were the most agonizing five days of my life. It's even hard to think about it now while I write this. Yet one thing I've learned over the years as a Christian is that the Bible says, **"The Lord is close to the brokenhearted and saves those who are crushed in spirit"** Psalm 34:18 (NIV).

We prayed continuously for a miracle. I called my pastor to ask him if terminating a pregnancy at twenty weeks was considered an abortion or not. I knew how I viewed abortion, and we were totally against it, but I had to search my soul and ask for wisdom to know if terminating this pregnancy at twenty weeks was wrong or right.

Thank God we didn't have to decide to abort because on May 12th, we went for another ultrasound, and a miracle happened! What happened next was literally the power of prayer in full force! The doctor walked in and sat us down. He said, "We now see part of your son's brain, and there is a sixty percent chance of him surviving." We were ecstatic and amazed at what God did! **"What do you mean, 'If I can'?" Jesus asked. "Anything is possible if a person believes"** Mark 9:23 (NLT).

We were so relieved and shocked at the same time! We called everyone we knew to tell them the wonderful news, and that is when we decided to make Andrew's middle name, James, after the Bible verse James 1:2 (NIV): **"Consider it pure joy, my brothers and sisters, whenever you face trials of many kinds."** We knew there would still be trials ahead with this pregnancy, but we were optimistic because he went from having a zero percent chance to live to a sixty percent chance. We praised Jesus!

It was mind-blowing to look back at the Hope in Numbers for both of those days. May 7th (5/7) was the day the doctor said Andrew had a zero percent chance to live, and May 12th (5/12) was the day the doctor said he had a sixty percent chance to live. The Hope in Numbers for 5/12 says, **"For you bless the godly, O Lord; you surround them with your shield of love"** Psalms 5:12 (NLT). It's amazing how God was looking down and surrounding us with His love at this time in our lives.

God blessed us when our son, Andrew James Wickert, was born on June 26, 2008 (6/26/2008). The Hope in Numbers for that day is 6/26, Psalm 62:6 (NLT), which says, **"He alone is my rock and my salvation, my fortress where I will not be shaken."** I remember how difficult it was to hear that news as a parent. I held onto a few promises from God during that time which kept my faith strong. **"They do not fear bad news; they confidently trust the LORD to care for them"** (Psalm 112:7 NLT), and **"for we walk by faith, not by sight"** 2 Corinthians 5:7 (ESV). These verses kept me going during those times of uncertainty and fear. God's Word became my fortress!

I say all of this for a few reasons. One, I love my son, Andrew, and I wanted to share his story with you in this book. Two, I know if my son, Andrew, could grow physically, mentally, and spiritually, he would give his best effort. He would love to have the ability to try Hope in Numbers. He might have even more Bible verses memorized than I! Unfortunately, with his physical and mental disabilities, he hasn't been able to develop properly and must remain in a wheelchair as special needs for the remainder of his life.

On the other hand, if you read this book, you can grow physically, mentally, and spiritually. Please, take full advantage of this opportunity God is giving you and try this gift. Again, not everybody gets the chance to do it. Make your life count and put your best foot forward to grow in all areas of life! And when you see my son Andrew in heaven one day, please be sure to let him know that his story inspired you to take on the journey of Hope in Numbers and give it a try! I know that would make him so very happy!

The Challenge

If you are willing to put this book to the test and try this out for yourself, I want to catapult you to success! Commit to trying Hope in Numbers for forty days and sign this page below. By signing this page, you will be committing to try Hope in Numbers and renewing your mind by memorizing scripture and searching for it in the world. I believe a commitment is a key to accomplishing anything worthwhile in life, and that is why I am asking you to do this for yourself. I want you to be abundantly blessed and fall deeper in love with Jesus every day!

For the 40-day commitment, I want to challenge you to memorize twelve verses in forty days. I made it easy for you by creating the "Every Hour I Need You" Challenge based on the hit song from Chris Tomlin. This activity is great because you will have a Bible verse memorized for every hour of the day when you need hope.

Here is how it works. Simply find these scriptures in your Bible or find ones that specifically speak to you, and write them down below! Just make sure you write one down for every hour of the day. Why write them down? Because writing them down will significantly help you to memorize them! I believe you can do this!

I will commit to practicing Hope in Numbers for 40 days:

Sign:_____
Date:_____

The Bible verse date this commitment was signed on:
_____
_____
_____

Hope in Numbers

The Every Hour I Need You Challenge

1 am/pm - Romans 1:16 _____
_____
_____
_____

2 am/pm - Galatians 2:21 _____
_____
_____
_____

3 am/pm - John 3:30 _____
_____
_____
_____

4 am/pm - Philippians 4:13 _____
_____
_____
_____

5 am/pm - 2 Corinthians 5:20 _____
_____
_____
_____

6 am/pm - Matthew 6:33 _____
_____
_____
_____

Chapter 2 - Try it

7 am/pm - Matthew 7:12 _____

_____

_____

_____

8 am/pm - Romans 8:31 _____

_____

_____

_____

9 am/pm - Mark 9:23 _____

_____

_____

_____

10 am/pm - John 10:10 _____

_____

_____

_____

11 am/pm - Hebrews 11:01 _____

_____

_____

_____

12 am/pm - Romans 12:02 _____

_____

_____

_____

CHAPTER 3 - RENEW IT

Now that you are committed to trying Hope in Numbers and understand that it takes the right attitude, I believe you will start falling in love with this way of living by faith! Hope in Numbers will start changing every activity you do for the better. Drives to work or school will never be the same because you are reminded of God's Word on every license plate, speed limit sign, and time of day. Watching sports on television will become a family Bible study for you to recall scripture together when you see jersey numbers and scores. Hope in Numbers leads to daily blessings!

Let's continue to the second step of this practice with the acronym T.**R**.U.T.H. and move on to the letter "R", which represents the "RENEW IT". We must renew our minds with God's Word. Being renewed is part of the Christian transformation process. We go from a life of sin and thinking about sin, to being renewed in mind and spirit and thinking about Jesus and His Word. Another theme Bible verse for Hope in Numbers is: **"Do not conform to the pattern of this world, but be transformed by the renewing of your mind. Then you will be able to test and approve what God's will is—his good, pleasing and perfect will"** Romans 12:2 (NIV).

I often like to say a particular phrase: "Get wrecked!" I say that phrase with a purpose beyond just the love of saying it. When I say get wrecked, I essentially mean renew your mind. Think about it this way. When a construction company has a job to rebuild a building, it must hire a wrecking crew to demolish the previous structure before the new one goes up. This same process happens in our minds and hearts when Jesus wants to build in us a stronger tower of faith. We must first get wrecked of our old belief patterns, doubts, and fears, before the new walls of faith go up. Jesus wants to build in us a new home of faith that is built to last on the unshakable rock of His promises.

While the world offers temporary shaky promises that can lose grip and fall away like the sand, God's promises are rocks built to last. Which promises are you looking to build your life with? Are you interested in building a sandcastle that can fall away in any moment? Or building a castle out of rock that will stand the test of time no matter the size of the waves that hit it?

Jesus is the Rock, the solid foundation that keeps our faith firm in a world that tries to shake us from our identity. A life with a foundation that is weak and cracked is one full of condemnation, guilt, and fear. That is a foundation that will be easily shaken and will not stand. **"If you do not stand firm in your faith, you will not stand at all"** Isaiah 7:9b (NIV). We must renew our minds, rebuild our faith on the solid rock-Jesus Christ, and not let our lives be built upon the shifting sand of this world. Hope in Numbers is the Extreme Makeover: Soul Edition! **"Because of God's grace to me, I have laid the foundation like an expert builder. Now others are building on it. But whoever is building on this foundation must be very careful. For no one can lay any foundation other than the one we already have—Jesus Christ"** 1 Corinthians 3:10-11 (NLT). Let's get wrecked for Jesus and remodel our lives on the rock that won't give way!

An American TV show that takes something old, worn out, and broken and transforms it into something that is new, functioning, and born-again is the popular MTV show from the early 2000s called *Pimp My Ride*. I used to enjoy watching and seeing this show and what amazing things they could do with old cars, trucks or vans. People would submit videos of their old, beat-up rides that had potential to be something in hopes of getting selected to get their ride "pimped". A rapper named Xzibit hosted the show, and he would surprise the owner by showing up at their house to get the keys.

After getting the keys, Xzibit would drive the vehicle to an auto shop called *West Coast Customs-* where the mechanics would begin transforming the vehicle into something unique that nobody had ever seen before! The show consisted of stripping the car of its old interior and anything broken or worn down. The car would be transformed, customized, and upgraded so that, when revealed, the owners could not recognize their vehicle. Sometimes the mechanics even ripped out the old engine and gave the owner a new one! Whatever work or upgrades the vehicle needed, they did. I'm talking new interior, custom paint job, and big rims. They always personalized the vehicle with out-of-this-world items for cars! I've seen cars that had 5 TVs in them, coffee machines, fish tanks, BBQs, tanning beds, and even a pool table in the bed of a truck!

At the end of the show, when the host Xzibit presented the new ride and a personalized gift, like a snowboard, guitar, etc., to the owner, he would say, "You need two things: the keys and you've officially been pimped!" As Xzibit pinched and released the shoulder sleeve of the owner's t-shirt, pronouncing that the owner is a newer and cooler person now! Seeing the transformation of these cars and watching the gratitude on the face of these owners was awesome, but you know what? God wants to do even greater work in your life! That's right, Jesus wants to pimp your life!

Jesus wants to upgrade, refurbish, and remodel your life in a way that turns your old, deteriorating faith into something new and exciting! He wants to give you a facelift of joy and upgrade your mindset so that you can **"be made new in the attitude of your minds"** Ephesians 4:23 (NIV). With this new, upgraded mindset, you can live out your days with faith that nobody has ever seen before! Jesus can do this through you with the gift of Hope in Numbers. How? Because you will be able to transform every number you see into a promise from God, inspiring others and lifting yourself. **"In the same way, let your light shine before others, that they may see your good deeds and glorify your Father in heaven"** Matthew 5:16 (NIV).

There was a great theologian back in the day, his name was P-Diddy, and he wrote a song titled "Mo' Money Mo' Problems". Well, Jesus told me once, "Mo' Bible verses you know, the fewer problems you have." I've been living this truth out daily, and it is one hundred percent accurate! My friends call me G-Diddy because I used to listen to and share rap music with my friends before I was a Christian. Now God has given me the wisdom to listen to His Word. Now, I share worship songs and sermons with my friends! So, if I ever get the pleasure to meet you in person, feel free to call me G-Diddy, and I'll be sure to share Jesus and Hope in Numbers with you!

Pray for the Gift

If you feel Hope in Numbers can change your life for the better and want to receive this gift, get ready, my friend! The most crucial step you can take to receive this gift is to pray and ask God for it. Our God is the Giver of gifts. When we ask for anything according to His will for our lives, He will deliver! **"This is the confidence we have in approaching God: that if we ask anything according to his will, he hears us"** 1 John 5:14 (NIV). I am confident that Jesus will deliver and answer your prayer today so that you can know His Word better and bring it with you everywhere you go!

If you are unsure how to pray for this spiritual gift, I will show you momentarily, but first, I want to explain why I believe it's appropriate for somebody to pray with you to receive a spiritual gift like this one. **"This is why I remind you to fan into flames the spiritual gift God gave you when I laid my hands on you"** 2 Timothy 1:6 (NLT).

There is a particular story found in 2 Kings Chapter 6 that is very interesting to me. There was a great prophet, Elisha, who was a messenger of God. Prophets are men who spoke by the guidance of the spirit. **"Holy men of God spoke as they were moved by the Holy Spirit."** 2 Peter 1:21 (NKJV). In today's world, we don't hear much about prophets, but we have holy men of God who are pastors that teach God's Word through the moving of the Holy Spirit.

In this story, the Israelites were in a battle against the Arameans- a strong army determined to defeat Israel. But, because he had such a strong connection with God, Elisha would know the very next move of the Arameans before it happened.

Hope in Numbers

With this valuable information, Elisha would inform the king of Israel of the location and time of the attack in advance.

Let's read a segment of scripture to find out what happens in this story:

> **The king of Aram became very upset over this. He called his officers together and demanded, "Which of you is the traitor? Who has been informing the king of Israel of my plans?" "It's not us, my lord the king," one of the officers replied. "Elisha, the prophet in Israel, tells the king of Israel even the words you speak in the privacy of your bedroom!" "Go and find out where he is," the king commanded, "so I can send troops to seize him." And the report came back: "Elisha is at Dothan." So one night the king of Aram sent a great army with many chariots and horses to surround the city. When the servant of the man of God got up and went out early the next morning, an army with horses and chariots had surrounded the city. "Oh no, my lord! What shall we do?" the servant asked. "Don't be afraid," the prophet answered. "Those who are with us are more than those who are with them." And Elisha prayed, "Open his eyes, Lord, so that he may see." Then the Lord opened the servant's eyes, and he looked and saw the hills full of horses and chariots of fire all around Elisha.**
> *2 Kings 6:11-17 (NIV).*

Now, that story gets me fired up! When people say that the Bible is boring, I want to say, *"You're boring!"* That story is straight life-wrecking-fire right there! Notice how Elisha prayed and asked the Lord to open his eyes and not send an army of angels on horses and chariots. This reveals the angels were already there! The battle was already in favor of the Israelites; they just couldn't see it yet! Once the prophet prayed over the man, he could finally see the supernatural favor and blessings the Lord had already prepared for them.

Do you see the parallel here with Hope in Numbers? Now, I am not comparing myself to a prophet, but I believe that once you pray for this gift, your eyes will start seeing the blessings and treasures in the world that have always existed. The numbers that have always been on your house, at your work, and on the streetcorners, will now turn into promises from God. Are you ready to experience this?

Let me help you pray to receive this gift, and let's watch Jesus bless your perspective and give you the gift of seeing numbers in a new and powerful way! Pray this prayer and receive it in your heart:

> *Father God, thank you so much for sharing this gift of Hope in Numbers with me. Lord, I desire to know your Word more and more each day. Your Word is a lamp unto my feet and is better than life itself. Lord, will you grant me the vision I need to start seeing your Word through numbers that I will see in the world? Lord, I ask you to open my eyes to see Holy Scripture through everyday interactions at home, on the streets, and anywhere else there are numbers. Transform my mind and give me the strong desire to retain these life-giving verses all the days of my life. May I never see numbers the same way again. In Jesus' name, Amen.*

Congratulations my friend! Your perspective is about to change forever. Now, every time you see a number, you will receive another dose of hope! Let me share with you the next step to transforming and renewing your mind.

Welcome the Transformation Daily

Now that we've prayed to receive this upgraded spiritual gift of seeing Hope in Numbers, I want to be honest with you. The complete renewal of your mind to see Hope in Numbers is a slow process. It's more of a crockpot gift than a microwave gift. In other words, it's not going to happen overnight, so I want to give you a fair warning because I don't want you to get discouraged that it doesn't happen quickly. Like anything worthwhile, it won't happen overnight. For example, you don't just go to the gym for a week and lose fifty pounds. You need to continually welcome this new lifestyle. Before you know it, results will appear! I know you can do this!

I cried out, "I am slipping!" but your unfailing love, O Lord, supported me. When doubts filled my mind, your comfort gave me renewed hope and cheer. *Psalm 94:18-19 (NLT).*

As kids, we learned about the morphing process of a caterpillar turning into a butterfly. The process begins when a hungry caterpillar hatches from an egg and lives a life feeding on as many leaves as it can. Once the caterpillar is nice and plump from feeding on leaves, it will cocoon itself upside down on a twig or a leaf. Within a period, the caterpillar morphs into a beautiful, new creature with wings and can soar! It's an amazing process.

A similar wondrous process happens when we transform to see Hope in Numbers. At first, progress will be slow, like a caterpillar moving toward its next meal. It might feel like you are not getting anywhere, but I encourage you to keep feeding on God's Word and memorize your scriptures. Then one day, when you are ready to fly, you'll morph into something beautiful that will soar to great heights! This gift will be your own, and you will start retaining many Bible verses and seeing them everywhere you go.

Retain Your Renewed Hope

When you are renewing your mind into seeing Hope in Numbers by memorizing Bible verses, you are essentially burning scripture into your memory and storing them in your heart forever. **"But the seed on good soil stands for those with a noble and good heart, who hear the word, retain it, and by persevering produce a crop"** Luke 8:15 (NIV). This verse means that there is very little value in merely hearing the Word of God and a day or so later forgetting what it says. We find true value in retaining your renewed hope by remembering the scriptures so that it changes who you are, what you believe, and how you act in different situations.

Hope in Numbers can help! If you desire to produce a great spiritual harvest in your heart, you must start to retain the Word by keeping it in your mind and storing it in your heart! Then you will have the reassurance of God's promises as they come to pass in your life.

Retaining God's Word keeps our lives moving with God's will and our calling as children of Faith. **"For we walk by faith, not by sight"** 2 Corinthians 5:7 (NIV). When I'm in a challenging season of my life, God's Word keeps my life in a biblical perspective. I have been filled with joy on so many occasions because of the gift of Hope in Numbers. It has consistently reminded me of a verse at just the right time. It's quite simply because God's Word can speak to me through numbers, and wherever God's Word is heard, it carries with it the power to move mountains! **"So faith comes from hearing, and hearing through the word of Christ"** Romans 10:17 (ESV). God can speak the same way to you!

Hear a testimony from my close friend, Trevor Santor, who started practicing Hope in Numbers just two years ago:

Hope in Numbers

When I first met Gordon, I was blown away at how much of a blessing it was to be around him. Literally, he was the first person I've ever met who was a living, breathing, walking Bible! He knew so many Bible verses by heart about things like my birthday, the current date, the time of day, and so much more! I knew he had a special gift, but I didn't know that I could someday have this gift as well.

Gordon kept trying to convince me that I could see Hope in Numbers and do exactly what he was doing. I wanted to be able to do it, but I really didn't think I was able to. Slowly, I started with one verse, Romans 8:31: If God is for us, who can be against us? He said I could find this number out in the world and be reminded of the verse.

Lo and behold. I started to see it! I remembered seeing it in the morning when it was 8:31 a.m. and again at night when it turned 8:31 p.m. It was like my mind knew when 8:31 was coming, and I would be reminded to look at the time and be blessed with the Bible reference. It was so crazy how it started to happen more and more frequently, like seeing it on license plates and grocery receipts. I loved the confidence the verse gave me so much that I wanted to unlock more of God's promises in my life. I then memorized my birthday Bible verse which is 2 Corinthians 5:17, then Romans 8:1, which is my favorite verse. Now I am to the point where I have over fifty Bible verses memorized and stored in my heart wherever I go.

This gift of Hope in Numbers has literally changed my life for the better. Now instead of hearing the thoughts and voice of the enemy, I am being constantly transformed and guided by God's Word and wisdom. This is the best practice to live out faith in Christ and fall in love with God's Word over and over again. Thank you, Gordon!

Your friend in Christ,

Trevor Santor

Trevor is a true inspiration to me and many others who will take on this Hope in Numbers journey for real! He took a bold step of faith and believed in me when I assured him that he could do Hope in Numbers. Now, to my readers: I want you to know the same thing that Trevor found out. You, too, can do this! Just start small. Renew your mind daily with Hope in Numbers and retain those verses.

Let me explain the concept of retaining with an analogy of wearing braces for your teeth. After years of wearing braces, and you get them taken off, do you hope your teeth stay straight? Nope. You get fit with a retainer that you wear at night to keep your teeth straight! When I was a teenager, I wore braces, and, as of right now, two of my beautiful daughters, Ky and Emily, both wear braces. The reason we get braces is so we can have straight teeth and carry a confident smile. Here's the most important thing: Once you get the braces off, wear a retainer to keep your teeth in alignment and prevent them from becoming crooked. Some people are like me and lose the discipline of wearing a retainer, and their teeth go back to being crooked again. I didn't wear my retainer for my teeth, but I wear my spiritual retainer by remembering God's Word. **"Consider what God has done: Who can straighten what he has made crooked?"** Ecclesiastes 7:13 (NIV). I hope you will wear God's retainer of His Word because you will carry with you so much confidence!

This analogy of wearing braces and your retainer fits well with the Hope in Numbers mission because that's what we do when we memorize Bible verses! When we know Bible verses and are reminded of them throughout the day at school, work, or home watching TV, it's like God's invisible retainer for our minds. **"In all your ways submit to him, and he will make your paths straight"** Proverbs 3:6 (NIV).

Unfortunately, if we don't retain verses, we forget them and miss the blessing of always having them with us. I'm sure you can relate when you go to church and hear a great message that inspires you to act, and you wish you could remember it all week long or for the rest of your life. Yet, we often forget the message or scriptures the next hour, day, or week! With Hope in Numbers, you can remember those scriptures that move you, and you can take those promises with you everywhere you go— from the church to the streets, from your home to the school, from the Bible study to the field. Hope in Numbers brings church with you Monday through Saturday.

God gives us such practical advice in the book of James when it says, **"Do not merely listen to the word, and so deceive yourselves. Do what it says. Anyone who listens to the word but does not do what it says is like someone who looks at his face in a mirror and, after looking at himself, goes away and immediately forgets what he looks like. But whoever looks intently into the perfect law that gives freedom, and continues in it—not forgetting what they have heard, but doing it—they will be blessed in what they do"** James 1:22-25 (NIV). Let's be a generation of Christians who sees God's perfect law and does not forget! Let's retain God's Word and put it into practice when it matters the most! Hope in Numbers will help you accomplish this through making cool stories and connections with the numbers of some of your favorite Bible verses.

The Power of Making Connections

It's been a crazy journey writing this book. It seems like the devil has had a target on my back from the moment I started writing it. As soon as I catch momentum writing the book, something tragic tends to happen that slows me down. The first incident was on December 20, 2016 (12/20/2016), when my son, Andrew, was rushed to the emergency room after having trouble breathing. I quickly drove to the hospital, praying and listening to worship music along the way because I knew that would give me strength. When I got to the hospital, I witnessed eleven doctors and nurses surrounding my son, Andrew, to try to keep him alive. There is no way of explaining this, but I didn't feel worried, fearful, or doubtful. Instead, I felt incredible confidence and trusted in the Lord because I knew that Jesus would show up again in this. And again, He did!

Andrew was in the hospital for a month and a half straight before being released with a full recovery. I almost feel like I'm living the book of Job at times because Job was a man who was on fire for God and wanted to live out his calling boldly. The enemy had other ideas for Job, wanting to stop him by doing anything he could to slow him down. The story in the Bible talks about how the enemy took away Job's family, his livestock, and his physical well-being.

I started to get a little more momentum moving forward with the book, but another night shortly after Andrew's incident, I was feeling discouraged. So I grabbed my phone and went on Instagram Live, where host a Hope in Numbers Live show. My followers on Instagram get on and engage with me as I share Hope in Numbers stories, Birthday Bible verses, and more. Instagram is a cool platform where I get to preach and encourage people. On this night, I had worship music playing in the background on shuffle, and the song I Can Only Imagine by MercyMe came on. I told my audience how this particular song increased my fire for the Lord when it first came out. The song is about imagining the moment you come face to face with Jesus. It's beautiful. I encourage you to listen to it.

Here's where things got crazy. As that song played during my Instagram Live show, I received a text from my Aunt Jan. It read, "Grandpa Alvin has passed away." When I read this, my heart sank, and I looked around the room, contemplating my next move. That is when I saw a wooden painting sitting there with this Bible verse written out on it: **"'For I know the plans I have for you,' declares the LORD, 'plans to prosper you and not to harm you, plans to give you hope and a future'"** Jeremiah 29:11 (NIV). On a separate piece of wood right next to that Bible verse was part of a desk we were going to sell at our next yard sale. Small writing the on the desk revealed the company Alvin crafted it. Literally—I can't make this stuff up. I was sitting by my grandpa's name on a piece of wood and an amazing Bible verse. This little situation gave me great peace because I knew my grandpa was experiencing what was sung in the song. My Grandpa Alvin was meeting our Savior, Jesus Christ, face to face, and it brought me tears of overwhelming joy!

My Aunt Jan later asked me if I knew the Bible verse that coordinated with the time of day when he died, 12:15 a.m. I replied to her with Romans 12:15 (NIV)**: "Rejoice with those who rejoice; mourn with those who mourn."** That is what my family was doing that next week as we packed our bags and flew to Canada to attend the funeral of my Grandpa Alvin. I've learned that when you rejoice with those who rejoice, you double the gladness, and when you mourn with those who mourn, you cut the mourning in half. So, we left to mourn with my family and be with my Grandma Kelly, who was married to Alvin for sixty-six years. The verse 1 Timothy 6:6 (NIV) is the perfect picture of their marriage together— **"But godliness with contentment is great gain."** They lived one of the most content, godly marriages I had ever seen in my whole life. My goal is to be like them and be happy as they were.

When we arrived at the funeral, I didn't know I would be asked to speak in front of my grandpa's entire church congregation about his life. Yet, when I got up in front of the 200+ people in the church, I wasn't nervous. What's my secret? I quoted Hebrews 10:35 to myself before going up on stage, and I knew Jesus would speak through me and wreck lives forever! **"So do not throw away your confidence; it will be richly rewarded"** Hebrews 10:35 (NIV). That's the promise I held onto, and boy, did Jesus deliver!

I went up there on behalf of the grandkids and shared with everyone the awesome experiences we had as grandchildren of Alvin Ross. I reminisced on how he used to love playing all kinds of card games with us, how much he enjoyed taking us to the Saskatchewan Roughrider football games, and how he always gave us money to buy ketchup chips that you can only buy in Canada! Those were my favorite memories!

After a while, I shared my grandpa's Birthday Bible verse. May 1st is his Birthday. **"Follow God's example, therefore, as dearly loved children"** Ephesians 5:1 (NIV). That's exactly how my grandpa lived life, as an example of Jesus. That verse went so well with Alvin's life, and it really touched the hearts of those who knew him. I got to share the Bible verse that goes with the day he died, January 27th: **"Whatever happens, conduct yourselves in a manner worthy of the gospel of Christ. Then, whether I come and see you or only hear about you in my absence, I will know that you stand firm in the one Spirit, striving together as one for the faith of the gospel"** Philippians 1:27 (NIV). My grandpa completed the race, and all in attendance knew he was with Jesus in heaven, smiling down on us. That gave us great joy.

After my talk about my grandpa's life and referencing a few Hope in Numbers, I received some incredible feedback from the congregation and other family members. In fact, I literally had a line of people waiting to talk to me to find out what their Birthday Bible verse was and to learn more about how Hope in Numbers works! They even asked me where I preach every week. That's funny! I should have told them at Discover Card! Do you see how this gift can be such a great evangelism tool too?

Make the Connection

Here is an interesting analogy that will significantly help you on your Hope in Numbers journey! This practice is all about making connections, and if you miss your connections, you will not get where you want to go, which is to God's blessings and will for your life! The analogy comes from the event following the funeral. When it was time to leave Canada, we tried to board our first flight from Saskatchewan to Calgary, where we had a connecting flight back home to Arizona. It was snowing so much in Saskatchewan that our flight got delayed five hours! When we finally got to Calgary, five hours late, we had missed our connecting flight home. We were bummed because we ended up staying the night at the airport and flying out the next morning. It was quite miserable!

Through the missed flight, God showed me if you miss the connections in your life to His Word, it can put a lot of stress on you, and you won't get to where you want to go. God once again used my bad experience to turn it around for good. **"And we know that in all things God works for the good of those who love him, who have been called according to his purpose"** Romans 8:28 (NIV).

Here's how connections work. To memorize any Bible verse with the book, chapter, verse number, and scripture, you must make connections that stick for you! If you don't make a strong connection in your mind, the odds of you memorizing verses diminish. It's like when you meet a new person for the first time, and you want to remember the person's name afterward. The simple trick is to make a connection with someone or something with which you are already familiar! For example, let's say you meet a guy named Nick. How do you remember his name without him having to tell you over and over again? You make a new, strong connection with this person and something familiar. Maybe Nick has a beard, and you can connect him with Santa Claus, Old Saint Nicholas. Pretty random, I know, but it works! You'll remember it! Whatever you must do to easily trigger a connection is the name of the game.

Do You Really Know the Bible?

Some people say they "know the Bible" and "know Jesus". That's kind of like pointing to the United States on a map and saying, "I know a guy who lives here!" That's not specific at all and wouldn't help navigate somebody if you were giving someone directions to get there. Some people can say, "I know a guy who lives here…" as they point to the state of Arizona on a map. That would be like somebody who knows that a Bible verse comes from a specific book in the Bible, like the Book of Romans. That's pretty good, but if somebody says, "I know a guy who lives on 5379 W. Charles Rd. Phoenix, Arizona 85309." That person is like somebody who knows a particular verse is from the Bible, knows the book it is in, knows the chapter, and the exact verse number! That is somebody who intimately knows that person and knows exactly where to find him! Don't you want to be like that with Jesus and His Word?

Are you starting to see the power in this? Knowing the exact Bible verse and its location in the Bible creates clarity! You will intimately know and find God's promises when you need them the most! **"For the kingdom of God is not a matter of talk but of power"** 1 Corinthians 4:20 (NIV). I will teach you how to make these strong connections and remember these powerful promises so that you will know them, use them and see them out in the world!

Connect 4

It works like this. You need to connect four elements of scripture for this to work well, like in the board game, Connect 4. If you've ever played it before, you know you connect four pieces to win. Bible memorization works like this. First, you make a connection with a verse in the Bible that you want to memorize. Second, you make a connection and memorize which book, chapter, and verse number it is found. Third, you memorize the actual words of the verse. Fourth, you connect with the author, God, so that you can understand the meaning of the verse and apply it to your life. If you can connect all four of these elements, then you win!

When you make a new connection, you win because you have added a link to the chain of the armor of God that we wear as Christians. **"Finally, be strong in the Lord and in his mighty power. Put on the full armor of God, so that you can take your stand against the devil's schemes"** Ephesians 6:10-11 (NIV). By memorizing the promises of God and storing them in your heart and mind so that they are ready to be used, you win the connect 4 of Hope In Numbers.

Let's look at a quick example. Say we want to memorize Philippians 4:4 because it is a verse that jumped off the page for you. Okay, great! That is the first step. Second, we memorize and make a connection with the book Philippians, the chapter, and verse number- 4:4. Third, we sit and memorize the verse word for word. **"Rejoice in the Lord always. I will say it again:**

Chapter 3 - Renew it

Rejoice!" Philippians 4:4 (NIV). Lastly, we connect with God and discover the meaning and purpose of the verse so we can apply it to our lives.

The process of connecting four doesn't always happen fast, but you will get better at it. Making these four connections is vital for growing spiritually with Hope in Numbers. This practice will help you really get to know Jesus through His Word. You will be able to memorize many Bible verses that will truly bless your life as you walk them out!

Here's where the fun starts. Once you make the four connections with a Bible verse, you start seeing that number in the world. When you see it, it will bring to memory the entire connection for you. The four connections will become one instant reminder! For example, when I see a 4x4 on a 4-wheel drive truck, I instantly envision Philippians 4:4 in my mind, and the words of the verse are instantly brought to my memory. Blessings will follow you everywhere as you start connecting God's Word with numbers.

Connections with Numbers

Believe it or not, you have already made many connections with numbers. We make many relationships with numbers throughout our lives. We all have birthdays, phone numbers, ages, home addresses, heights, weights, favorite holidays, etc. Let's play a game and see how many connections you can make with the numbers I give you. Here you go 911, 365, 12/25, 24/7, 316.

Well, how did you do? How many connections did you make? I'm sure you made most, if not all, of these connections. Let's review. 911 is the emergency telephone number in the United States, 365 is the number of days in a calendar year, 12/25 is Christmas Day, 24/7 is the hours in a day and days in a week, and 316 is John 3:16, one of the most recognized verses from the Bible. The point is you already have a numbers-connecting mechanism working. We can tap into it further and maximize our memory bank by filling it with God's wonderful Word. Here is how you can make connections with these examples.

First, 911 is a phone number people call when they feel in danger or need emergency help. Here is how you can make a connection to a promise from God. Psalm 91:1 (NIV) says, **"Whoever dwells in the shelter of the Most High will rest in the shadow of the Almighty."** When you call 911, you are likely to need protection and safety, and a shelter is a structure that provides those things. So, there is a new connection you can make! **"Shelter of the Most High."** After you call 911 and help comes to your rescue, you usually feel at rest. That is a new connection for the last part of the verse that says "…will rest in the shadow of the Almighty." When you see 911, you can think of shelter and rest because that is what emergency rescue comes to provide you. Once you have a new, solid connection with the scripture, it becomes much easier to remember the verse!

Next, look at the number 365, the number of days in a year. Let's connect it to Psalm 36:5 (NIV) **"Your love, Lord, reaches to the heavens, your faithfulness to the skies."** Okay, awesome! Let's connect this verse to its number. This verse talks about the love and faithfulness of the Lord reaching to the heavens and skies. Well, here is how I would make a connection. I remember that the Lord loves me and is always faithful to me, 365 days a year! He has never failed me yet! You can also picture a calendar that you hang on a wall with beautiful pictures of the heavens to help you remember that this verse talks about the heavens and the skies. You can then remember the word "reaching" because when the month changes on a calendar, you have to "reach" up to switch to the next month. These are just a few suggestions that you can use for remembering this verse, but making connections is all

Chapter 3 - Renew it

very personal. Whatever ideas, imagery, or personal experiences help you to make the strongest connections are the ones you should use! That is the real key to memorizing and making connections. Make memories with these verses. A unique and personal connection will be the strongest connection.

Awesome work making these new connections! Let's attempt 12/25, Christmas Day! For most, Christmas morning can be a very joyful experience as families gather around the Christmas tree to open presents. For other families, it is more chaotic than anything. Here is a connection you can make with the date 12/25 from the book of **Matthew "Jesus knew their thoughts and said to them, 'Every kingdom divided against itself will be ruined, and every city or household divided against itself will not stand.'"** Matthew 12:25 (NIV). With this particular verse, you can make a few different connections:

One connection could be about the part of the verse that says, **"Jesus knew their thoughts and said to them..."** When you think about Christmas, many young kids believe in Santa Claus, who claims to know if you've been bad or good. We know Jesus is the true reason for the season, and Jesus actually knew their thoughts to be bad or good! You can also make a simple connection by thinking about Christmas morning with the family. A household divided against itself will not stand or enjoy Christmas together! Do you see how this works? This is how you make simple connections that will stick with you and last!

Another great example is 24/7. When you look at the verse in Jeremiah 24:7 (NIV), **"I will give them a heart to know me, that I am the Lord. They will be my people, and I will be their God, for they will return to me with all their heart."** This verse mentions the heart two times in the same verse. You can make the connection that your heart beats every day without skipping a beat. Your heart beats 24/7. That connection can make it easy to

Hope in Numbers

remember that the verse mentions the heart. The middle part of the verse: **"they will be my people and I will be their God"**, can be remembered when you think that God does not take days off from being our God. Twenty-four hours per day, seven days per week, we are His people, and He is our God! It's mind-boggling how we can form a simple connection, which makes it way easier to remember and trigger these powerful scriptures from memory! Try a few on your own, and you will be blown away by how easy memorizing a promise from God can be!

The last example is 316, which is a number that many Christians have seen and even know by heart; it comes from John 3:16 (NIV), **"For God so loved the world that he gave his one and only Son, that whoever believes in him shall not perish but have eternal life."** You may have seen a sports fan on TV holding up a sign at a game with the number 3:16 on it. It's the most popular Hope in Numbers and a powerful verse for people who know it. People seem to know it by heart because it is a cornerstone verse that summarizes the Gospel into one simple yet profound sentence. I could tell you how to make a connection with this verse, but I figure you already have this one down. Plus, I would rather tell you about an amazing Hope in Numbers story that happened with this number!

Hope in Numbers Stories

One of my favorite athletes in our current sports era is Tim Tebow. Mostly because he is a sold-out Christian, and it's refreshing to see such a good role model in the sports world. He has such an incredible Hope in Numbers story that shows how God used numbers from a highly televised football game to bring glory to the name of Jesus! Here's what happened. When Tim Tebow played college football for the Florida Gators, his team made it to the National Championship in 2006. Before that game, Tim decided to paint "John 3:16" on his eye black under his eyes. In the end, he was the winning quarterback of that game. But much more incredible than that was because of Tim 94 million people googled "John 3:16" that day and read the scripture that summarized the entire Gospel of Jesus Christ in one verse. Now that's a huge win!

Fast forward three years from the day the Florida Gators won the national championship, and Tim Tebow is the starting quarterback in the NFL playing for the Denver Broncos in a playoff game against the Pittsburgh Steelers. The game ends with Tim Tebow throwing a winning touchdown pass to secure the victory for his team. It was an incredible performance, but what was revealed after the game was so spectacular that only our sovereign God could have orchestrated it.

The Denver Broncos public relations guy went up to Tebow and asked him with a big smile, "Tim, do you realize what happened?" Tim thought he was talking about the football game and who they would play next week. Then this man told Tebow, "No, I don't think you realize, today is three years since you wore 'John 3:16' under your eyes. In today's game, you threw for 316 yards, your yards per rush were 3.16, your yards per catch were 31.6, the ratings for the game were 31.6, and the time of possession was 31.6!"

Again, about 90 million people googled "John 3:16". It became a trending topic on Twitter. When asked about all the matching numbers for 316, Tebow said, "Some say it's a coincidence. I say - BIG GOD." That is why I love Tim Tebow!

I agree with Tim Tebow here. People call these random coincidences. However, I'm one hundred percent convinced they're not just random happenstances but a sign from God that He's with us everywhere we go. Jesus said, "I'm with you always," and Jesus made everything in existence, including numbers. If

Hope in Numbers

you use numbers to find hope, you'll experience tons of your Hope in Number moments and stories, which will keep you on fire for the Lord!

I have had hundreds of unbelievable God moments using this gift of Hope in Numbers, just like Tim Tebow experienced after winning that playoff game. These moments reveal that God wants to encourage us through His Word and what He has done for us. I'm going to share with you some other amazing Hope in Numbers stories to show you more about how God inspired me and others at just the right moment to see His Word through numbers.

11:34

Back in the early 2000s, my pastor at the time, Brian Anderson from Vineyard Church of North Phoenix, challenged me to memorize one Bible verse per week for fifty-two weeks. If I stuck to the plan, by the end of the year, I would have fifty-two Bible verses memorized. I liked the sound of that, so I accepted the challenge! I fell so in love with memorizing Bible verses that instead of memorizing just one verse per week, I started memorizing one verse per day!

The first ever Bible verse I memorized, besides the well-known John 3:16, was Jeremiah 29:11. Soon after keeping that promise with me forever, I memorized Galatians 2:20, Proverbs 3:5-6, Matthew 6:33, Joshua 1:8-9, 1 John 1:9, Romans 8:31 and so forth. Yet, I'll never forget my first Hope in Numbers story, which occurred with 1 Corinthians 13:4.

How I would decide on a verse to memorize happened from one of two occurrences: one, I would be reading my Bible, and a verse would jump right off the page and meet me where I was at currently, or two, a pastor from the stage would preach on a powerful scripture, and I would say to myself, *I need this verse in my soul forever!*

One day, I was at a friend's wedding, and the pastor who officiated preached using the most famous Bible verse about love. He started to quote, **"Love is patient, love is kind. It does not envy, it does not boast, it is not proud. It does not dishonor others, it is not self-seeking, it is not easily angered, it keeps no record of wrongs. Love does not delight in evil but rejoices with the truth. It always protects, always trusts, always hopes, always perseveres. Love never fails"** 1 Corinthians 13:4-8a (NIV). I thought, wow, I need to remember this truth ASAP and apply it to my love life! During this time, I was in my early 20's, single, and preparing to be a good husband one day. You're welcome, honey!

Before the wedding finished, I memorized all four and a half verses that described how real biblical love looked. Later that night, I was winding down and lying down on my bed. Looking at the clock next to me, I saw it was 11:34 p.m. I quickly made the connection of 1 Corinthians 13:4, the verse that I had just memorized. But what happened next blew my mind. Remember, I was lying on my bed, my head turned sideways. So, while I could still see it read 11:34, I could also see how it looked upside-down. It read "hEll" when it was upside down.

I then got this revelation, I believe, from the Lord Himself. He said to me, "I wrote the truth about real love in 1 Corinthians 13:4 because that is the way true love should be, but if you do the opposite and flip it by being impatient, rude, self-seeking, easily angered, and keep every record of wrong, then you will experience hell on earth." I've told this Hope in Numbers story to hundreds of people, and they fully agree with this wisdom. If you take biblical love and turn it upside down, you will experience a version of hell in your relationships.

Hope in Numbers

11:34 Compatibility Test

Here's a fun test to see if the person you're dating, engaged to, or married to is causing hell in your life or not. Is the person more of an 11:34 person or an upside-down, hell-causing person? Look at the activity below. On the left is the true definition of biblical love from 1 Corinthians 13:4-7. I want you to add the person's name you are with first. Check the box on the left if you can honestly say they have biblical love activated and put an X in the box if they do not pass the test. Then I want you to examine yourself. Take inventory and find out who or what is causing hell on earth in your relationship. If you need to work on some things, that's completely fine. If you both pass, you should probably call a pastor and get married soon if you are not already!

1 Corinthians 13:4 Other Person Compatibility Test

☐ Love is patient - _____ is patient.

☐ Love is kind - _____ is kind.

☐ Love does not envy - _____ does not envy.

☐ Love does not boast - _____ does not boast.

☐ Love is not proud - _____ is not proud.

☐ Love does not dishonor others - _____
_____ does not dishonor others.

☐ Love is not self-seeking - _____
_____ is not self-seeking.

☐ Love is not easily angered - _____
_____ is not easily angered.

☐ Love keeps no record of wrongs - _____
_____ keeps no record of wrongs.

Chapter 3 - Renew it

- ☐ Love does not delight in evil but rejoices with the truth - _____.
- ☐ Love always protects - _____ always protects.
- ☐ Love always trusts - _____ always trusts.
- ☐ Love always hopes - _____ always hopes.
- ☐ Love always perseveres - _____ always perseveres.

1 Corinthians 13:4 My Compatibility Test

- ☐ Love is patient - _____ is patient.
- ☐ Love is kind - _____ is kind.
- ☐ Love does not envy - _____ does not envy.
- ☐ Love does not boast - _____ does not boast.
- ☐ Love is not proud - _____ is not proud.

Hope in Numbers

- ☐ Love does not dishonor others - _____
_____ does not dishonor others.

- ☐ Love is not self-seeking - _____
_____ is not self-seeking.

- ☐ Love is not easily angered - _____
_____ is not easily angered.

- ☐ Love keeps no record of wrongs - _____
_____ keeps no record of wrongs.

- ☐ Love does not delight in evil but rejoices with the truth -
_____ .

- ☐ Love always protects - _____
_____
_____ always protects.

- ☐ Love always trusts - _____
_____
_____ always trusts.

- ☐ Love always hopes - _____
_____
_____ always hopes.

- ☐ Love always perseveres - _____
_____
_____ always perseveres.

The Legal Disclosure of Hope

I have another unforgettable Hope in Numbers story I'd like to share with you so you can see how this works in real life before you experience it on your own! Over the last eighteen

Chapter 3 - Renew it

years of working at Discover Card, I have read aloud thousands of legal disclosures verbatim on the phone with customers. One disclosure that I read when I was working in the fraud department is one that I will never forget.

I had one of the worst stat months ever. I failed seven of my last fifteen calls that were being monitored for quality purposes. I was discouraged, and the management team was thrilled with my performance. For some reason, I would forget what to say at the right time. I was stressed because fraud activity was picking up with the holiday season. I was beating myself up for making these little mistakes over the phone until Jesus revealed one of the most fire Hope in Numbers stories to date!

Customers would call to have their cards closed due to fraudulent activity. The legal disclosure I would read to them was: "It will take 4 to 6 business days to receive your new card and up to 10 days to receive the fraud credits." Call after call, I would have to say this exact line, and I kept messing up the call. Little did I know, the verse I needed was hidden in those numbers! Psalm 46:10 (NLT) says, **"Be still, and know that I am God!"** I needed this advice. To lean not on my strength and wisdom but on His!

From that day forward, I quoted Psalm 46:10, and it changed my attitude and perspective for each future call I received. I stopped failing calls because I held onto this promise from Psalm 46:10. I became more confident and courageous, knowing that I serve a mighty God who guides me through His Word! **"Your statutes are my delight; they are my counselors"** Psalm 119:24 (NIV).

Hope in an Instant

I want you to know that not all Hope in Numbers stories will be that in-depth or hard to find. Sometimes they are way simpler

Hope in Numbers

to find and will bring instant joy to remember for a lifetime. For example, around the Thanksgiving holiday one year, my girls and I set out to go shopping and buy a pumpkin pie and toys for Christmas. We went to our local supermarket and went down the aisle where they had pumpkin pies and BOOM! Immediately, I saw a Hope in Numbers promise that brought me instant joy! The price tag on the pumpkin pie was $3.48, which reminded me of this verse, Psalm 34:8 (NLT) **"Taste and see that the Lord is good. Oh, the joys of those who take refuge in him!"** We surely did taste and see how good the Lord is. Of course, we also tasted the pumpkin pie that the verse was on!

It was entertaining to see the correlation between that verse and the pumpkin pie. I was curious to know what other Hope in Numbers I could find that made sense with the product and the price tag. So we went to the toys section of the store and saw a large Power Ranger toy that had all the Power Ranger characters together in their vehicle fortress. The price tag was $49.00. Another powerful verse came to my mind without pulling out my Bible—Ecclesiastes 4:9 (NLT): **"Two people are better off than one, for they can help each other succeed."** Again, this verse coordinated beautifully with the product and its label. The Power Rangers were successful because they worked together as a team.

Here's what the rest of the passage says in Ecclesiastes 4:10-12 (NLT): **"If one person falls, the other can reach out and help. But someone who falls alone is in real trouble. Likewise, two people lying close together can keep each other warm. But how can one be warm alone? A person standing alone can be attacked and defeated, but two can stand back-to-back and conquer. Three are even better, for a triple-braided cord is not easily broken."** I believe the Power Rangers group was victorious in their battles because the more people you have that support

Chapter 3 - Renew it

you, the greater chance you have of succeeding! The Word of God is full of amazing truths and powerful wisdom like this.

Another memory was when my girls and I went shopping and saw a life-sized Darth Vader action figure in the toys section. The price on it was $99.00, and again it quickly brought to mind a well-connected Bible verse, this time from the book of Daniel. The verse says, **"But the Lord our God is merciful and forgiving, even though we have rebelled against him"** Daniel 9:9 (NLT). It was such an interesting connection because Darth Vader is part of the Rebellion in the Star Wars series! These were incredible connections that I will never forget! I was experiencing Hope in Numbers and was making memories with God's Word and my kids; nothing better!

I have one more relevant and inspiring Hope in Numbers story. When I was driving home one day from work, I passed our local In and Out Burger. The address of the building was 828, and it gave me some inspired wisdom. Jesus revealed in that moment that people will come in and out of your life but take heart because Romans 8:28 (NIV) says, **"And we know that in all things God works for the good of those who love him, who have been called according to his purpose."** Now that is Godly wisdom I know to be true in my life!

Hear a quick testimony from a friend in Christ, Ryan, who has given Hope in Numbers a real opportunity to change his perspective see the world through the lens of God's Word:

> *God desires for us to see Him in everything we do. There could not be a better explanation than that for Hope In Numbers, as it is exactly what it teaches you to do! It retrains your thought process and focus to see everything through God's eyes. Suddenly the time on the clock, a passing gas station price board, and spreadsheet numbers at work remind you of God's words through scripture. It*

will start small by helping you memorize verses here and there. Before you know it, you won't be able to stop the fire that consumes inside you to see it at all times. It is a new and refreshing way to retain and remember the most important teachings of our lives.

Gordon was given a special gift that he is now sharing with the world to be shared by all, and I could not be more excited! This technique has the power to change EVERYTHING!

"Do not conform to the pattern of this world, but be transformed by the renewing of your mind. Then you will be able to test and approve what God's will is—his good, pleasing, and perfect will." -Romans 12:2

This book will TRANSFORM you, and you will NEVER be the same! In fact, when I just sent Gordon my testimony, you won't believe what happened. I emailed him my testimony at 12:02 pm, and Gordon responded, "Did you plan to send it at that time because that's the exact time that matches the Bible verse you talked about in your testimony?"

"WOW," I responded, "No, I didn't, but God did."

I hope people will start seeing God's Word in many numbers they see, like Ryan. When you renew your mind to see Hope in Numbers, you can create memorable Hope in Numbers stories and experiences them for yourself. I would love to hear about them. When you start having some of your own stories, let me know about them. Post them to social media anywhere and use the hashtag #Hopeinnumbersstories so that others can hear them too!

Chapter 3 - Renew it

Connect 4 Challenge

This challenge is designed to help you continue your journey and memorize powerful verses with numbers familiar to you. This fun activity will help you build an arsenal of verses! Fill in the blanks with a correlating verse you can memorize and connect 4!

Birthday -_____ = Bible verse _____
_____
_____
_____

Age -_____ = Bible verse _____
_____
_____
_____

Height -_____ = Bible verse _____
_____
_____
_____

Phone number -_____ = Bible verse _____
_____
_____
_____

Address -_____ = Bible verse _____
_____
_____
_____

Hope in Numbers

License plate number -_____ = Bible verse _____
_____
_____

Favorite number -_____ = Bible verse _____
_____
_____

Favorite sports players jersey number -_____ = Bible verse _____
_____
_____

Your jersey number -_____ = Bible verse _____
_____
_____

Time you wake up every day -____ = Bible verse _____
_____
_____

First number you see after reading this -_____ = Bible verse _____
_____
_____

CHAPTER 4 – USE IT

Let's continue to the third step of our practice with the acronym T.R.**U**.T.H. and move on to the letter "U", which represents the word "USE". Let's start first with a true story that will help you see the importance of putting this value of knowing God's Word to use in your life.

When the Oakland A's baseball team ended their season in 1990, the financial officers attempted to balance the books. To their surprise, they were in a surplus of one million dollars! They thought, "How could this be?" Their suspicions rose to that of Ricky Henderson as they looked over their numbers to find out how. They found out there was a check to Ricky Henderson for one million dollars that never got cashed.

They called up Mr. Henderson to find out what happened to the check. When they called Ricky, he knew where it was. It was in a picture frame hanging on the wall in his house as a constant reminder that he was a millionaire. Not really, though, because he didn't cash it in yet! They suggested that Ricky make a copy of the check, hang it on the wall, and cash in the real one to receive the actual dollar amount.

That was a true story of a man who did not cash in a promise. I feel that this is what we do as Christians sometimes with the promises made by God for our spiritual wellness. We aren't cashing into the storehouse of blessings and treasures from His Word like we could be. I see Christians all the time with tattoos of Bible verses on their bodies or decorations hanging on their walls, but they miss the part of meditating on the Word, living it out daily, and receiving the value of the scripture.

We aren't always cashing in God's promises, but with Hope in Numbers, we will have the key to unlocking the many promises everywhere we go! It's almost as if there are hidden treasure boxes around us, and people walk right by these treasures of joy and blessings. Hope in Numbers gives you the all-access key to the many blessings and promises from God's Word! **"In him lie hidden all the treasures of wisdom and knowledge"** Colossians 2:3 (NLT).

G-O-D Caching

There's a new activity in the recent days of smartphone apps and technology spreading worldwide called geocaching. Geocaching is basically a global treasure hunt for random items hidden in different places. People can hide something inside a box or Tupperware at a particular location around town and then set the coordinates on an app with a GPS. Other people then log into the app and see where people have placed certain 'caches' for them to find. Once somebody finds the cache, they record their findings inside a log and put the item back where they found it or replace it with something else for another person to find. It's a fun new craze going around, but just for entertainment. The items have little or no value other than the surprise of seeing what other people think to put inside their cache. My family and I love geocaching, especially when traveling to different places on vacation or around town.

What if, instead of geocaching items with little to no value, we G-O-D cache into promises with eternal value? That is the blessing of Hope in Numbers, my friend! We treasure-hunt for God's promises every day so that our faith can continue to grow and get stronger. **"I rejoice in your word like one who discovers a great treasure"** Psalm 119:162 (NLT). When life gets hectic, you can always slow down and find promises from God to help you win the battles that come your way. His promises are literally in every number you see throughout the day. Just look around you and find some numbers nearby.

You can level up your spiritual life and get in the game by memorizing more and more Bible verses! Be inspired to collect the Words of God and not the toys of men! **"Do not store up for yourselves treasures on earth, where moths and vermin destroy, and where thieves break in and steal. But store up for yourselves treasures in heaven, where moths and vermin do not destroy, and where thieves do not break in and steal. For where your treasure is, there your heart will be also"** Matthew 6:19-21 (NIV).

Unlock the Box

Just like the Ricky Henderson story, if you have a Bible verse on a tattoo or hanging up on your wall, but you're not applying it to your life, it is like having a locked treasure box in your possession that you aren't able to open and receive what's inside. Jesus is the source of all these treasures and blessings, and He wants His family of believers to be able to unlock the many promises and receive them into our lives. He gives us wisdom here when He says, **"'My mother and my brothers are all those who hear God's word and obey it.'"** Luke 8:21 (NIV). To hear God's Word and obey it, we need to be reminded of it and apply it daily. That is how we unlock the promises and receive the treasures hidden all around us as believers in Christ!

Numbers are the treasure boxes, and to unlock these treasure boxes, we must complete the task of memorizing scripture. Memorization is the key to unlocking these promises when we find them out in the world. If you can connect 4, as we talked about in the previous chapter, then you, my friend, have the opportunity to gather a storehouse of spiritual wealth to store in your heart. **"I have hidden your word in my heart that I might not sin against you"** Psalm 119:11 (NIV). As Christians who live in the world, we might not ever become sinless, but with God's Word hidden in our hearts, we will sin less and less. This is what Hope in Numbers can help you accomplish!

When I am out in the world G-O-D caching and searching for hope and a word from God, I call it "Treasure Hunting for Hope". I even started a hashtag on social media, **#TreasureHunt4Hope**, to use when somebody finds an awesome verse and photographs or videos the number out in the world and knows the scripture that goes with it. BOOM! They have unlocked the treasure box and are now sharing it with their friends and family through social media!

I encourage you to go on your own treasure hunt while G-O-D caching for hope and post your findings on social media with the hashtag **#TreasureHunt4Hope**. You can also see what other people have found out in the world. It might just bless your life forever!

Missing Child

Remember back in the day when milk cartons used to print missing child ads on them? Nowadays, you might see a missing child ad in a local newspaper or on news television, but can we be honest for a minute? Although a sad and tragic situation, those missing child ads have never sent me on a wild search and rescue mission for that child. I've recently asked myself the question, why? If I lost my child, I would wish everybody would stop what they were doing and look for them; However, unfortunately, that isn't the case.

I believe this is true because if it isn't your child that is missing, you don't feel like you've lost anything. If you feel you haven't lost anything or anybody, you won't search for it. It sounds selfish, but I think most of us respond that way. On the other hand, if it is your child or my child who was missing, we would not rest until we found our child. When your valuable possession is lost, the desire to find and get it back burns deep inside!

Let me ask you a question. What if I was to tell you that something valuable of yours is lost right this moment? Something that God has given all of us, but only a few people have found it. Most people look for it in all of the wrong places. Here's the truth. Most people have lost hope and do not know where to find it. They look to their careers, more money, nice cars, or big houses, but they find emptiness. Why is that?

God created us for something much more meaningful— a deep and intimate relationship with Him that only He can fulfill. **"Call to me and I will answer you, and will tell you great and hidden things that you have not known"** Jeremiah 33:3 (ESV). God will answer our call and reveal His amazing promises and wisdom from His Word. He will point us to where our hope and everlasting joy have been waiting this entire time, in His precious Son, Jesus!

Hope in Numbers

Jesus beautifully illustrates what He does if something of value ever goes missing from His possession—He goes out immediately to find it! One parable is about a lost sheep. Jesus says, **"If a man has a hundred sheep and one of them gets lost, what will he do? Won't he leave the ninety-nine others in the wilderness and go to search for the one that is lost until he finds it? And when he has found it, he will joyfully carry it home on his shoulders"** Luke 15:4-5 (NLT). If you have lost hope in your life, put everything else on hold and get it back!

Jesus further illustrates His point by telling the parable of the lost coin. **"Or suppose a woman has ten silver coins and loses one. Won't she light a lamp and sweep the entire house and search carefully until she finds it? And when she finds it, she will call in her friends and neighbors and say, 'Rejoice with me because I have found my lost coin'"** Luke 15:8-9 (NIV). As I was writing this section of the book, my wife was frantically turning the house upside down and sweeping because she lost the center diamond of her wedding ring and was trying to find it. She eventually found it the next day; I was excited about not having to replace it, but the message here is this: why aren't we frantically searching for our lost hope? God's Word provides all the hope we need every day, and we can now find it everywhere we go with the practice of Hope in Numbers.

Let's not let the worries of this world keep us from attaining the hope that is meant for us to hold. God wants us to remain close to His heart and call for our lives. We can surely get closer by knowing His Word and seeing it out in the world to be reminded daily. Find your hope with Hope in Numbers today, tomorrow, and for the rest of your days!

An Anchor for Your Soul

Have you ever felt distant from God? Much further away than you'd like to be? Or that you drifted away from God's Word, and your faith seems to have turned to doubt? Well, my friend, let me tell you that you are not alone, and I have a great solution for you!

A tremendous benefit of practicing Hope in Numbers is that it can be a stronghold and an anchor for your soul! When you are seeing, recognizing, and using God's Word daily through Hope in Numbers, you will have an unlimited source of encouragement, motivation, wisdom, truth, and purpose that will anchor your soul close to the Lord by keeping you firmly planted to His Word. **"My advice is wholesome. There is nothing devious or crooked in it"** Proverbs 8:8 (NLT).

Like a boat on the open sea, drifting back and forth, rocked by unprecedented waves, you need a lifeline and an anchor keeping you tied down and safe. Hope in Numbers provides an unbreakable lifeline tied to the rock of God's unshakable Word. **"This hope is a strong and trustworthy anchor for our souls"** Hebrews 6:19a (NLT). This anchor will keep you safe, secure, and harnessed with peace in times of turbulence. **"I have told you these things, so that in me you may have peace. In this world you will have trouble. But take heart! I have overcome the world"** John 16:33 (NIV).

I can't tell you how often the Word of God has kept me from drifting away from a life of righteousness and returning to old patterns. There have been so many times that God's truths and promises have overpowered the deceitfulness of Satan's lies. I hold near and dear to this truth found in Hebrews 2:1 (NLT): **"So we must listen very carefully to the truth we have heard, or we may drift away from it."** Hope in Numbers helps us to keep from drifting away. We are simply one number and one truth away from regaining our focus and pursuit back on Jesus, the Perfecter of our faith. **"Cling to your faith in Christ, and keep your conscience clear. For some people have deliberately**

violated their consciences; as a result, their faith has been shipwrecked" 1 Timothy 1:19 (NLT). If you keep your life anchored to the Word of God, you can avoid a life shipwrecked by the loss of hope, faith, and purpose.

Worship Music For My Soul

One of the best ways I get close and in God's presence is through listening to worship music. I believe that God wants us to live on fire for Him daily. I do this by putting on my headphones, which I call my Devil Beats, daily and blasting worship music all day. I call them Devil Beats because I wear the headphone brand Beats by Dre, and I like to think of my headphones to blast out the devil and his schemes. I listen to sermons and worship music during most of my day, and it's hard for the devil's thoughts to stay in my head for long, let alone get in my head when I have a steady flow of Christian music and sermons nourishing my mind and soul.

A bonus of Hope in Numbers is that when you have a variety of Bible verses memorized, you start to recognize the scriptures sung in many worship songs. It's a great way to use Hope in Numbers because almost every worship song is on life-wrecking scriptures found in the Bible! The more verses you start to memorize, the more you recognize them in worship songs. A great way to practice Hope in Numbers is when you can hear and sing these scriptures and know where they are coming from in the Bible. When you hear a chorus or a line in a song from a Bible verse, you have even more joy in your heart because you know that you know it!

This makes worship music even more exciting and praiseworthy than it already is because not only will you recognize the verse in the song, but you will recognize that the verse is inside of YOU! Now that is a reason to praise God! I will give some examples of great songs based on powerful scripture passages.

The first example comes from the song "To Live is Christ" by Sidewalk Prophets, the lyrics, *"for me to live is Christ... for me to live is Christ... for me to live is Christ to die is gain"* come straight from Philippians 1:21—**"For to me, to live is Christ and to die is gain."** Singing scripture is a very powerful way to let it sink into your soul. This is a very beneficial practice to help you use the scriptures you have memorized.

In the song "The Way" by Housefires, the lyrics say, "I believe You are my fortress, You are my portion, You are my hiding place, I believe You are the way the truth, the life, I believe You are the way, the truth, the life." Those lyrics come straight from John 14:6 (NLT), **"Jesus told him, 'I am the way, the truth, and the life. No one can come to the Father except through me.'"**

In the song "Mighty Warrior" by Elevation Worship, the lyrics are "Our God a mighty warrior, you're a consuming fire, In victory you reign, We triumph in your name, Jesus the great commander, You conquered death forever, In victory you reign, We triumph in your name. Those lyrics about God being a consuming fire come straight from Hebrews 12:29 (NIV): **"For our God is a consuming fire."**

In the song "Let There Be Light" by Hillsong Worship, the lyrics say, "Good news embracing the poor, comfort for all those who mourn, for the broken hearted, we sing louder. Release from prison and shame, oppression turning to praise, for every captive sing louder. Restoring sight to the blind, breaking the curse of the night, for all in darkness sing louder. Proclaiming freedom for all, this is the day of the Lord, beauty for ashes." Those lyrics come straight from Luke 4:18-19 (NIV) when Jesus says, **"'The Spirit of the Lord is on me, because he has anointed me to**

Hope in Numbers

proclaim good news to the poor. He has sent me to proclaim freedom for the prisoners and recovery of sight for the blind, to set the oppressed free, to proclaim the year of the Lord's favor.'" The last line, "beauty for ashes" comes from Isaiah 61:3a (NLT): **"To all who mourn in Israel, he will give a crown of beauty for ashes."**

In the song "Let There Be Light" by Hillsong Worship, the lyrics say, "Good news embracing the poor, comfort for all those who mourn, for the broken-hearted, we sing louder. Release from prison and shame, oppression turning to praise, for every captive sing louder. Restoring sight to the blind, breaking the curse of the night, for all in darkness sing louder. Proclaiming freedom for all, this is the day of the Lord, beauty for ashes." Those lyrics come straight from Luke 4:18-19 (NIV) when Jesus says, **"'The Spirit of the Lord is on me, because he has anointed me to proclaim good news to the poor. He has sent me to proclaim freedom for the prisoners and recovery of sight for the blind, to set the oppressed free, to proclaim the year of the Lord's favor.'"** The last line, "beauty for ashes," comes from Isaiah 61:3a (NLT): **"To all who mourn in Israel, he will give a crown of beauty for ashes."**

In the song "Whom Shall I Fear [God of Angel Armies]" by Chris Tomlin, the lyrics say, "And nothing formed against me shall stand. You hold the whole world in your hands. I'm holding onto Your promises. You are faithful. You are faithful." The lyrics "and nothing formed against me shall stand" come straight from Isaiah 54:17 (KJV): **"No weapon that is formed against thee shall prosper,"** and that line, "I'm holding onto Your promises," sounds a lot like the acronym for Hope In Numbers—Holding Onto Promises Everywhere. Boom!

I have a quick challenge for you to try and come up with songs you know and see if you can connect some of the lyrics to any Bible verse you know!

Chapter 4 - Use it

Song Name = _____
Band Name = _____
Lyric = _____
_____

Bible Verse = _____
_____
_____

Song Name = _____
Band Name = _____
Lyric = _____
_____

Bible Verse = _____
_____
_____

Song Name = _____
Band Name = _____
Lyric = _____
_____

Bible Verse = _____
_____
_____

Song Name = _____
Band Name = _____
Lyric = _____
_____

Bible Verse = _____
_____
_____

If you are new to Christian music and need somewhere to start, here is the list of my top 20 favorite Christian bands and my favorite song from each. Please look up these songs and more of their songs on YouTube or however you listen to music. Ask God to speak to you during these songs and watch him move mountains in your life! They will also help you to fall more and more in love with Jesus, I promise!

1. Song – "Resurrecting" Band- Elevation Worship
2. Song – "Let There Be Light" Band- Hillsong Worship
3. Song – "Jesus" Band- Chris Tomlin
4. Song – "All My Hope" Band- Crowder
5. Song – "First" Band- Laruen Daigle
6. Song – "The Way" Band- Housefires
7. Song – "I Can Only Imagine" Band- Mercy Me
8. Song – "Great Light of the World" Band- Bebo Norman
9. Song - "Live Like That" Band - Sidewalk Prophets
10. Song – "No Longer Slaves" Band- Bethel Music
11. Song – "I Have This Hope" Band- Tenth Avenue North
12. Song – "If We are the Body" Band- Casting Crowns
13. Song – "Chain Breaker" Band- Zach Williams
14. Song – "Forgiveness" Band- Matthew West
15. Song – "Take You Back" Band- Jeremy Camp
16. Song – "This is Amazing Grace" Band- Phil Wickham
17. Song – "Oh Father" Band- CCV Music
18. Song – "I Am Healed" Band- Dianne Michelle
19. Song – "The Rock Won't Move" Band- Vertical Worship
20. Song – "Rusty Nails" Band- 7eventh Time Down

Inject your Soul with Hope in Numbers Daily

In 1991, when I was just ten years old, an incident changed my life forever. It was a typical day. I was drinking my usual 7-Up soda as part of my daily routine. I started not feeling so well, and it worsened throughout the day. I drank the whole liter of 7-Up, which had tons of sugar in it, and I started throwing up. I thought maybe I had the flu, but then I started to black out, and I knew these were not normal symptoms of the common flu.

When my mom came home, I told her how I was feeling. She told me I was probably diabetic. She's a nurse, so I believed her. When I went to the hospital, my blood sugar level was 751, which is extremely high! A normal blood sugar level is between 80-120. That day, the doctor confirmed that I had juvenile diabetes, or type 1 diabetes. I would need to take three to six shots of insulin and four to eight finger pricks per day just to stay alive. The 751 blood sugar level also has some Hope in Numbers significance for me. It says in Psalms 75:1 (NIV): **"We praise you, God, we praise you, for your Name is near; people tell of your wonderful deeds."** God keeps me alive because He is not done with me yet. He continues fulfilling my mission and calling of teaching the world this gift of Hope in Numbers. That is why I continue to praise Him and tell everyone I know how wonderful He is!

Type 1 diabetes is a chronic condition where the pancreas produces little or no insulin. I've had it for the past twenty-six years, and it has no known cure. The only healing is heaven and the one day when I get a new body! But for now, I must inject my body with insulin every day to stay alive. A healthy person produces insulin, a hormone that allows sugar (glucose) to enter cells to produce energy from within the body. I have to manage my blood sugar levels by injecting insulin and keeping a close watch on my diet and lifestyle to prevent major complications or death.

I've had to take thousands of injections over the last twenty-six years, but now I have an insulin pump hooked up to my stomach that constantly gives me insulin to keep my sugar levels

101

balanced. The insulin pump tells me my basal rate. The basal rate is the rate of continuous supply of insulin injected into my body all day long. Then there is a function on my pump called a bolus, a large dose of insulin given by injection. Bolus rapidly achieves the therapeutic concentration needed in the bloodstream. Those are the two ways I take insulin: through the basal rate giving me insulin continuously, and bolus every time I eat a meal and need a large dose of insulin to hit my bloodstream quickly and balance me.

I tell you this because Jesus gave me a revelation: sin is a deadly disease like diabetes. Diabetes is currently the third most deadly disease in the USA, but sin trumps diabetes because it carries eternal ramifications. We must inject our souls with the promises from God, so we can fight against the temptation to sin. We need daily doses of basal-rate Bible verses to keep our spirits high throughout the day and bolus Bible verses ready when we need a larger dose of God's Word when our spiritual temperature is low. **"The spirit is willing, but the flesh is weak"** Matthew 26:41b (NIV).

Some basal rate Bible verses that can help you stay on fire for the Lord and continuously bless you all day long are **"Surely your goodness and unfailing love will pursue me all the days of my life, and I will live in the house of the Lord forever"** Psalm 23:6 (NLT) or **"Great is his faithfulness; his mercies begin afresh each morning"** Lamentations 3:23 (NLT) or **"Walk with the wise and become wise, for a companion of fools suffers harm"** Proverbs 13:20 (NIV).

Or maybe it's urgent, and your temptation level is rising. You need some spiritual strength to get through it. Now would be a good time for some powerful bolus Bible verses to get you back to spiritual balance. One verse that brings me back to balance is 1 Corinthians 2:9 (NIV): **"However, as it is written: 'What**

no eye has seen, what no ear has heard, and what no human mind has conceived —the things God has prepared for those who love him." A verse like that can bring a quenched spirit back on fire for the Lord because of God's amazing grace and love for you.

Or you might need to extinguish a flaming arrow of lust that shot your way so you can quickly bring 2 Timothy 2:22 (NLT) to mind: **"Run from anything that stimulates youthful lusts. Instead, pursue righteous living, faithfulness, love, and peace. Enjoy the companionship of those who call on the Lord with pure hearts."** If that doesn't work, you can recall James 4:7 (NIV): **"Submit yourselves, then, to God. Resist the devil, and he will flee from you."** These verses can give you a clear path on how to resist these temptations that want you to give in to the detriment of your purity. God's Word is powerful enough to provide you with a way out!

As you can see, I've found a message and strength in my diabetes and can use it for good against the enemy's attacks in my spiritual walk. Having a theme bible verse for my diabetes helps me never give up even though my body is trying to kill me every day. **"Therefore, we do not lose heart. Though outwardly we are wasting away, yet inwardly we are being renewed day by day"** 2 Corinthians 4:16 (NIV). I keep the number 416 close to my heart every day, reminding me of this powerful promise from God. Thank you, Lord, for the courage you give me every day through Hope in Numbers!

Active Faith

For years I've had an IV in my stomach that injects me hourly with insulin to balance my sugar levels. As the Apostle Paul talks about, I basically have a thorn in my side. I take insulin and inject it into my body, but one thing to note is insulin doesn't always lower your blood sugar all at once; it can take hours to take effect. When I take insulin, my pump tells me how many units of insulin are active in my body so that I don't take too much. The function of my insulin pumps is called Active Insulin.

For me, Hope in Numbers helps me to have Active Faith in my life. Sometimes the verse doesn't take effect right away in your life. Nevertheless, keep it in your heart, and it will start to take effect! You need a lot of Active Faith to be a follower of Jesus! Like it says in James 2:17 (ESV): **"So also faith by itself, if it does not have works, is dead."**

Using Hope in Numbers in your daily life will help you take your Bible on the go in this busy, self-seeking world in which we live. Seeing Hope in Numbers and using it in your daily routine will satisfy your soul and help you take your faith to a higher level! **"What good is it, dear brothers and sisters, if you say you have faith but don't show it by your actions?"** James 2:14 (NLT). An action propelled from a changed heart is real faith in action. These actions are not from duty or religion but from the righteous desire to serve God and others.

My favorite NBA basketball player, Stephen Curry from the Golden State Warriors, believes in the above Bible verses in James so much he helped get the "Active Faith" clothing brand off the ground. Active Faith is a popular Christian sports apparel company that I love and support. Curry preaches that having active faith in your Christian walk is like actively practicing and playing basketball to become one of the greatest basketball players and shooters of all time. He has put in thousands of training and practicing hours to become the best basketball player.

The truth is that Jesus did not come to save us to become the chosen frozen. Jesus wants us to move and make our faith come alive and active so that we use it and bless others with our faith. Like a can of paint, it is useless until we open it, stick a paintbrush in, and apply paint to a wall. Then it becomes active, and we can see the results of a beautifully painted wall!

Our Bibles are nice to have, but they will not be a resource for us until we open them up and activate the words inside by applying them to our lives. Then we will see God's provision. Here's a powerful formula for you to utilize in your own Bible study routine: Memorization + Application = Transformation.

Don't Let the Fire Expire
I'm sure you've experienced hearing a sermon or verse preached such that you caught revelation, and then a week or so later, you have forgotten all about it. I'm here to implore you- do not let that happen in your life any longer! Take full advantage when the Word is alive and well in your life! As that fire is burning inside of you to read the Bible, memorize verses, and use your faith boldly, continue in it! Do not let the fire expire.

There are expiration dates on most things in life. In the food department, there are expiration dates on items like milk, bread, and cheese. These items can be good and tasty for you to eat when they are ripe and in season. But when the expiration date passes, they are no longer of benefit and have to be thrown out. Other things in life have expiration dates, like relationships and even your life on earth. We live a fleeting life. We have some relationships now that we won't have in ten years. We are going through seasons now that will end. Make the impact that you can now while you still have the opportunity.

There are also expiration dates on spiritual revelations that you receive and ignite a fire from within you. Why not strike while the iron is hot? Do not delay activating your faith into bold action, a new commitment, or a righteous decision. **"'Does not my word burn like fire?' says the Lord"** Jeremiah 23:29a (NLT).

What's fantastic about Hope in Numbers is that God gives fresh revelation through His Word every day in different locations and situations. One day, you will need faith to lift you out of depression, and you can find hope in a timely verse that shows up. Another day, you will find Hope in Numbers that you can relay to a friend who has just gone through a terrible breakup. God gives you fresh verses to use to help people. Do not let it expire without using it and applying it to your life or somebody else's.

One Verse Can Cure You

One word from God can help you, encourage you, guide you, and even cure you from sin's deadly grip on your life; However, you must have the correct perspective on what the Bible verses are saying. Then you can watch it cure you in your hopeless situations! My pastor, Steven Furtick, says that your perspective is either your prison or your passport. Man, he is so right! I have lived in some prison perspectives before in my life. I'll share with you a couple of examples of how Jesus freed me from bondage once I received a word from God and had the correct perspective on what Jesus meant. You'll see that numbers had a lot to do with it too!

As you can imagine, after having my son, Andrew, in 2008, who was born with special needs and could possibly die at any moment, I slowly drifted away from my faith in God. I had major doubts about God and His love for our family. I was working at a church as an assistant youth pastor and serving the best I could, so how could God let this happen to us? I fell into a deep depression. For years I didn't tell anyone at all. I slept twelve hours a day, hurting and doubting like crazy because of Andrew's health issues. There was nothing I could do for my son, and as a dad, that broke my heart more than anything. I was broken and slowly drifting away from God.

I was so depressed about Andrew's health issues partly because I thought my past sins caused God to punish us; I was reaping what I sowed from a rebellious, sinful past. The Bible verse that cured me of this prison was so powerful. The moment I read this verse with the right perspective, I went from living daily in doubt and depression to instant faith and freedom! I was instantly healed with one verse!

My healing came immediately after reading John 9:1-5 (NLT): **"As Jesus was walking along, he saw a man who had been blind from birth. 'Rabbi,' his disciples asked him, 'why was this man born blind? Was it because of his own sins or his parents' sins?' 'It was not because of his sins or his parents' sins,' Jesus answered. 'This happened so the power of God could be seen in him. We must quickly carry out the tasks assigned us by the one who sent us. The night is coming, and then no one can work. But while I am here in the world, I am the light of the world.'"**

Hallelujah! Thank you, Jesus, for your Word! John 9:3 answered my most pressing question that was causing all my doubts. I thought my sin caused what happened to my son, Andrew, but that's not the case. It happened so the power of God could be seen in him. If you've ever met my son, you know he is priceless! His smile and joy are infectious, and I hope you meet him one day to see his unbelievably joyful countenance. Now, when I see the numbers 93 or 95, I'm instantly reminded of the Bible verses in John that cured me of my depression.

One thing you need to know about my son, Andrew, is he can't walk, talk or do much on his own because of his condition. He also has poor vision, so he likes watching movies on his iPad close to his face. His all-time favorite movie is the original, Cars. He loves the voices of the race car characters, Lightning McQueen and Mater. They bring him so much comfort. It's so cute to hear

Andrew laugh when he thinks it's funny. Andrew has probably watched the movie Cars a thousand times, and it never gets old.

We've bought Andrew tons of Cars toys and posters. We even bought him a Cars bed of Lightning McQueen for his room. Sometimes, he and I have sleepovers, and I sleep with him. I'm over six feet tall. That's how big this Cars bed is. One of the coolest Hope in Numbers stories happened while I was writing this book. My Hope in Numbers office is in my son's room by his huge Cars bed. One night while writing, Jesus revealed something that made me cry like a baby. My son sleeps in this huge Lightning McQueen Cars bed that he loves, and I noticed that the race car number for Lightning McQueen is #95! The Bible verses that healed me from depression were John 9:1-5. For over eight years, Andrews pretty much-watched Cars every day of his life, and Lighting McQueen's race car number was my freedom verse, but I couldn't see that until Jesus blessed my perspective of seeing hope in those numbers!

Let's read a testimony from my friend, Brian Goslee, from Cincinnati, Ohio, and how Hope in Numbers changed his perspective into seeing God's mighty hand working everything together for good!

> *About a year ago, I was introduced to a wonderful missionary for the Lord, Gordon Wickert. Most people, however, would not recognize that he is a missionary. He is a family man, works in the business world, volunteers as a youth group leader, and boldly teaches people how to see God's truth and the Word around them.*
>
> *Gordon is humble and on fire for Jesus, always. His mission is to "train the world to see God's promises everywhere" by teaching people how to see and memorize Bible verses from the numbers they encounter all around them every day, and it works!*

The best way to encourage you to start seeing Hope in Numbers is to share some stories of how it has worked in my life. The first thing I started doing after being shown Gordon's ministry was to look up Bible verses based on the time displayed on my microwave clock. I would think, "Oh, I see it's 5:14. I wonder if I can find a verse for that." Then I would literally start looking through all the 5:14 verses on my YouVersion app and see what I found— "You are the light of the world. A city on a hill cannot be hidden" Matthew 5:14 (ESV).

Next, I noticed numbers at the gas pump and on parking lot light posts. When I returned to that same gas pump, I remembered that verse: "And when he saw Jesus from afar, he ran and fell down before him" Mark 5:6 (ESV). I made some fun videos and passed them on to Gordon. This process of seeing Hope in Numbers in parking lots, on digital clocks, and in many other places continues to this day.

Once you get Hope in Numbers going, the verses and numbers seem to find you! Here is one example of what I mean. I was on a reading plan that was taking me through Psalms and read an awesome verse that I underlined: "As the mountains surround Jerusalem, so the Lord surrounds His people, from this time forth and forevermore" Psalm 125:2 (NLT).

I found that to be an inspirational verse, and I memorized it. Afterward, I realized that could be my birthday verse since January 25th is my birthday!

But this next anecdote "takes the cake" almost literally. This is when I knew I was "eaten up" with Hope in

Numbers! My wife and I were at our anniversary dinner, celebrating and talking about various parts of our life and different ministry topics. The next thing we knew, we both were scrolling through the YouVersion Bible app, looking for a good anniversary verse for 6/27!

Yes, we were sitting in a nice restaurant on our 25th anniversary, looking for an anniversary Bible verse because we enjoy looking for Hope in Numbers. Call us crazy! But guess what? It made us start thinking about God and all of the promises that He has come through!

By the way, we finally found Matthew 6:27 (ESV): "And which one of you by being anxious can add a single hour to his span of life?"

My most recent stage has been to start memorizing larger sections of scripture because I have found that I enjoy getting God's Word deep into my mind and heart. I was inspired by Gordon's ability to memorize entire chapters of the Bible. It is not about having a stunt to impress others, but it is about knowing part of God's Word so well that it becomes part of who you are. You are replacing sinful thoughts with God's thoughts, replacing the ways of the world with the ways of God.

The best way I can put it is this, daily practicing Hope in Numbers has changed how I live and see the world around me for the better! I think of God and pray 10, 20, or 30 times a day or more, all because of seeing Hope in Numbers. I encourage you to try it out today!

The Cure for Complete Rejection

In 2008, after having our miracle son, Andrew, born into this world with major complications, something bizarre happened. Andrew was in the NICU because he was born two months premature. One of the doctors came up to Andrew's mother and me and said, "You are likely going to get a divorce over this, you know? 9 out of 10 families divorce after having a special needs child." I was shocked that this comment came out of a doctor's mouth, but I laughed it off because divorce was never even an option for me. I made a promise to God that I would never file for divorce.

Long story short, in 2012, that doctor was right. My wife, at the time, hadn't made the same life-long commitment and gave me divorce papers. There was nothing I could do. She made her decision totally on her own and divorced me on July 23, 2012 (7/23/12). I felt utterly rejected. I was not the perfect husband by any means, but I didn't do anything biblically wrong to cause her to file for divorce. I'm not here to talk negatively about my ex-wife because she is an amazing mother to our two children, Emily, and Andrew. But, truthfully, I was forced into the divorce unwillingly and could do nothing about it. I was shipwrecked emotionally for some time until God healed me again. Here's how He did it.

God's Word is so powerful and is exactly why I am so on fire to help you to memorize it and see it everywhere you go! One verse can heal you from your bondage of sin, shame, and depression. Here are three Bible verses that helped me break out of one of the most difficult times in my life. I know they can help deliver somebody else who is reading this too. The first verse is from Proverbs 28:13 (NIV): **"Whoever conceals their sins does not prosper, but the one who confesses and renounces them finds mercy."** I knew I desperately needed God's mercy because

I was not prospering at all in my life. I was carrying around the heavy guilt and shame of being divorced for a long time, so I started confessing everything to God and asking for forgiveness.

This verse in Proverbs kept flooding my mind over and over after the divorce. I had it memorized years earlier, but God has a way of reminding you of His Word right when you need it if you put it to memory. I committed to writing all the sins I hid from my wife and other people down on paper. I went to everyone I hurt and lied to because of my sin, telling them I was sorry and asking them to forgive me. Some of them did. Others did not, but I felt a lot better afterward because I did what God asked me to do. It was amazing. I experienced the fresh start it talks about in Acts 3:19 (NIV): **"Repent, then, and turn to God, so that your sins may be wiped out, that times of refreshing may come from the Lord."** I promise you; this verse is true to the core! I was renewed, refreshed, and ready to live a life worthy of the call of Jesus Christ until the day I die! Are you ready to experience this for yourself? Your revival is awaiting you!

The next Bible verse that helped me tremendously get through my divorce was from Proverbs 15:1. This verse helped me turn what could have been an ugly divorce situation into one that was manageable and worked as best as it could. It says, **"A gentle answer turns away wrath, but a harsh word stirs up anger."** As you can imagine, the divorce stirred up in me all different emotions like anger, sadness, and hatred for getting rejected for no biblical reason.

I wrote many mean text messages I never sent because I was given wise advice from one of my best friends, Pastor Craig Beyer. He told me that when I get into a battle with my ex-wife and feel a fire burning in my heart, I have two options: to throw gas on the fire or throw water on it. When a conversation turns into a burning fire, what are you throwing on it? Gas or water?

My ex-wife and I get along well because that conversation helped me throw water on the fire ninety-five percent of the time to put out many of our disputes.

Since my ex-wife decided to leave me, I was the one who got the keep the house that my parents helped me buy. They helped me buy it because we lost our home to a short sale in 2008, and our credit score was poor after the housing market crash. At the time, we had a two-story house, which wouldn't work well with Andrew being in a wheelchair. So my parents decided to help out and purchase us a fixer-upper for really cheap. Little did I know the profound Hope in Numbers divinely placed in the home address.

My home address is 3019, and it was going to be great advice for me when my wife divorced me three years after buying it. Remember, at the time, Hope in Numbers wasn't conceived in my head yet, but you will see how faithful our God was by using scripture to bless me with hope. Deuteronomy 30:19 (NLT) says, **"Today I have given you the choice between life and death, between blessings and curses. Now I call on heaven and earth to witness the choice you make. Oh, that you would choose life so that you and your descendants might live!"** Those were the two choices I had when forced to divorce. I could have chosen life or death, blessings, or curses. My advice for people who get divorced is that you can either get bitter or get better because of it. I chose to get better and choose life and blessings by running to God for my refuge. Now I have a beautiful, blended family that lives under the same roof. God, you are truly amazing in all your ways!

Some of you reading this book may have experienced the pain and frustration of divorce. I pray that you haven't and never will experience it, but as a once-divorced man, I believe I felt a less, but similar, pain as Jesus felt when He was rejected by one of

Hope in Numbers

his disciples, Judas. Not only did Judas reject Jesus, but His own tribe of Jewish people demanded His crucifixion. This next Bible verse cured me of all hate, anger, and rage from the rejection I experienced. I've repeated this verse hundreds of times before, but I never really knew the depth of it until my divorce. Watch God work in mysterious ways!

The Bible verse that I repeated over and over says, **"Jesus said, 'Father, forgive them, for they do not know what they are doing.'"** Luke 23:24 (NIV). There is a lot of freedom in those words, my friend. Meditate on these words if anybody has ever done you wrong in the past, and I promise God will remove the prison bars to a new window of grace.

One day I was listening to Pastor Steven Furtick preach a message called "No More Nails". It was a message about how the devil has a hammer and tries to hammer you down and keep you there, but he now has NO MORE NAILS! The nails are all in the cross, **"Those who belong to Christ Jesus have nailed the passions and desires of their sinful nature to his cross and crucified them there"** Galatians 5:24 (NLT). During the message, Furtick quote the verse, **"Father, forgive them, for they do not know what they are doing"** found in Luke 23:34.

I was excited because that verse cured me of my feelings of rejection and erased all the angry thoughts about my ex-wife. I wanted to memorize the location, but I couldn't put my finger on how to memorize 23:34 until God revealed to me how, and I'll never forget it! Get this… 23:34 in military time is 11:34, and 11:34 is the Bible verse that talks about true biblical love that I mentioned earlier in the book! God made a connection for me that I'll never forget. These verses carry so much meaning in my personal life and freedom! Are you ready to experience some renewed hope in your life? I'm telling you, let God's Word start speaking to you through numbers!

50 First Dates

When my ex-wife asked for a divorce, I searched my soul to find out what happened in our marriage. How did I lose her? What did I do wrong? At the time, Jesus reminded me of this verse: **"So we must listen very carefully to the truth we have heard, or we may drift away from it"** Hebrews 2:1 (NLT). He gave me the answer right there in that passage. I had stopped listening to the voice of Truth and slowly drifted away from God and my spouse. It wasn't a big drift all at once. That's too noticeable. Instead, it was a slow, fading drift that was hard to recognize. I stopped reading my Bible daily, I forgot most of the Bible verses I had memorized when I was first on fire for the Lord, and I wasn't getting into the presence of God through worship music like I used to.

I drifted and lost the love I first had for God and my wife, but then remembered these verses: **"But I have this complaint against you. You don't love me or each other as you did at first! Look how far you have fallen! Turn back to me and do the works you did at first"** Revelation 2:4-5 (NLT). That is exactly what happened. What happened in my marriage and why I had lost my burning desire for the Lord became clear.

Do you remember that first love you had with God when He called you back into His embrace? You couldn't wait to arrive early to church so you wouldn't miss a single worship song or moment of an inspiring message. That first love when you took notes about the sermon and applied it immediately to your life. That first love was when you weren't afraid to sing your heart out during worship with your hands lifted high because you didn't care what others thought about you and your relationship with the Lord. Some of you may have experienced this first-hand or likely seen somebody else like this.

Maybe you can relate more to the love you had at first with your spouse. You remember at first how you couldn't stop thinking about them. You would stay up late and get up early just to hang out. You would do whatever they wanted because you didn't mind; you just wanted to spend time together. At first, you would get creative with all the ways you could show compassion to them, and your love grew and grew.

So let me ask you a question. What has happened since then? What has happened to that first love burning deep inside you for the Lord or your spouse? I believe God gave me the answer to this question with another analogy from the movie: *50 First Dates*. Public Service Announcement: I do not recommend this movie to Christians. I watched it before I became on fire for the Lord, but like most things, it does carry a message that God used to help me learn how to stay on fire for Him daily! Again, God showed me how He turns any messy situation into a message!

Here's how the storyline goes. A man named Henry Roth is deathly afraid of commitment. Until one day, he meets the beautiful Lucy Whitmore. They hit it off, and Henry thinks he's finally found the woman of his dreams. That is until he discovers she suffers from short-term memory loss because of a car accident. She forgets who Henry is every day, and he has to meet her for the first time every day. So, Henry comes up with a creative daily routine to make Lucy fall in love with him over and over again every single day.

Every day, Lucy does fall in love with Henry, and he asks her to marry him. Spoiler alert— she says yes! Henry knew that from that day forward, every day, he would have to make Lucy re-fall in love with him, and it would be worth it. I felt like God was telling me, "Exactly right, Gordon, you need to come up with a daily routine to re-fall in love with Me every day!"

"And you must love the Lord your God with all your heart, all your soul, and all your strength. And you must

commit yourselves wholeheartedly to these commands that I am giving you today. Repeat them again and again to your children. Talk about them when you are at home and when you are on the road, when you are going to bed and when you are getting up. Tie them to your hands and wear them on your forehead as reminders. Write them on the doorposts of your house and on your gates"** Deuteronomy 6:5-9 (NLT).

A daily routine is a key to awakening your soul and reigniting your love for God over and over again! There's nothing better in this world than when you have a daily routine that fills your heart with an abundance of peace and joy from the Lord! **"Rejoice in the Lord always. I will say it again: Rejoice!"** Philippians 4:4 (NIV). I will share with you the daily routine I have developed over the years. I hope it will encourage you to seek your routine so that you will fall in love with Jesus over and over again! This is one of the most life-changing habits I've ever formed as a believer in Christ.

Daily Routine

Every morning I set my alarm clock to wake me up at 5:01 a.m. to remind me of Ephesians 5:1 (NLT) **"Imitate God, therefore, in everything you do, because you are his dear children."** Then I walk to the restroom and turn on the faucet to wash my face. I take a glance at the soap bottle in my bathroom that has a big "11.25" on it for the number of fluid ounces it holds; it instantly reminds me of Proverbs 11:25 (NLT) **"The generous will prosper; those who refresh others will themselves be refreshed."** Those are two promises I hold onto every day because I see and think of them before I even leave my house in the morning.

my neighbor has the address 3023 in plain sight for me to see. This number refreshes my mind with a promise from Lamentations 3:23 (NLT) **"Great is his faithfulness; his mercies**

begin afresh each morning." Can you see how this routine reawakens my soul to prosper in the Lord? The armor of God is beginning to latch its way around me. As I continue on my drive to work, the first sign I see is a speed limit sign for 25 mph, and it instantly reminds me of Philippians 2:5 (NLT): **"You must have the same attitude that Christ Jesus had."** I get on the I-17 freeway for a few miles reminding me of 2 Timothy 1:7 (ESV): **"for God gave us a spirit not of fear but of power and love and self-control."** Seeing that verse makes my confidence and boldness level for the Lord rise to great heights! The speed limit sign on the freeway is 65 mph, bringing to mind Deuteronomy 6:5 (NIV): **"Love the Lord your God will all your heart and will all your soul and with all your strength."** This is how you can use Hope in Numbers for your daily routine. I'm not even to work yet, and my soul has been blessed by God's Word through my daily routine, not to mention all the different license plates I've seen along the way!

As I pass many exit signs on the freeway, I continue to get blessed by God's Word. One of my favorite exit signs is exit 212 because I see James 2:12 (NIV): **"Speak and act as those who are going to be judged by the law that gives freedom."** Then the exit I get off the freeway at exit 214, which brings Philippians 2:14-15 (NLT) to mind: **"Do everything without complaining and arguing, so that no one can criticize you. Live clean, innocent lives as children of God, shining like bright lights in a world full of crooked and perverse people."** I'm serious when I say my daily Hope in Numbers routine to work prepares me for my day ahead. It's like a morning Bible study on my route to work that suits me in the Armor of God.

When I get off the freeway, the first speed limit sign that I see is 35 mph which boldly speaks the wisdom to me in Proverbs 3:5 (NIV): **"Trust in the Lord with all your heart and lean not**

on your own understanding." As I pull into the parking lot at Discover Card, I look back to the freeway and see the freeway overpass with the numbers 14 ft.- 10 in. for how much space is available so that drivers know if they can get their truck through or not. But what I see is 1 Corinthians 4:10a (NIV) **"We are fools for Christ."** That's what I live by because we are either a fool for Christ or a fool for the world. Whose fool are you?

When I walk into the Discover Card building, I immediately see a 10 10 on the wall that reminds me of John 10:10 (NIV) **"The thief comes only to steal and kill and destroy; I have come that they may have life, and have it to the full."** At this point, I feel very blessed because I have God's word igniting my soul. Then I start working on hundreds of fraud cases. Something you might not know is every Discover Card number starts with 6011. Pull out your Discover Card if you have one, and look! When introduced to Hope in Numbers, Jesus reminded me that every time I see the number 6011 to think of Ephesians 6:11 (NIV) **"Put on the full armor of God, so that you can take your stand against the devil's schemes."** I have done this for years by having a Hope in Numbers routine on my way to work. You can start mapping out your today!

Daily Routine Challenge

Time your alarm clock goes off _____

am/pm + Hope in Numbers = _____

_____

_____

_____

_____

Hope in Numbers

A number you see in your house, bathroom, bedroom, etc. _____
+ Hope in Numbers = _____
_____
_____
_____

Neighbors address or license plate verse _____
+ Hope in Numbers = _____
_____
_____
_____

Any number you see in your vehicle _____
+ Hope in Numbers = _____
_____
_____
_____

First speed limit sign you see _____mph + Hope in Numbers =
_____
_____
_____

A Good St/Ave/Dr/Apt #, Freeway/Exit # you see _____
+ Hope in Numbers = _____
_____
_____

Chapter 4 - Use it

Any number you see along the way to school, work, etc. _____
+ Hope in Numbers = _____

_____
_____
_____

Any number you see at school, work, etc. _____
+ Hope in Numbers = _____

_____
_____
_____
_____

Any number you see_____
+ Hope in Numbers = _____

_____
_____
_____
_____

Any number you see_____
+ Hope in Numbers = _____

_____
_____
_____
_____

CHAPTER 5 - TEACH IT

Let's continue to the fourth step of our practice of the acronym T.R.U.T.H. and move on to the letter "T", which represents "TEACH IT". There's a great quote by Benjamin Franklin: "Tell me, and I forget, teach me, and I remember, involve me, and I learn." Teaching other people is an amazing practice that refines your skills and blesses other people at the same time! Teachers know this. When you have the responsibility to teach somebody else a concept, it helps you to learn and understand the concept on a much deeper level. Teaching others about Hope in Numbers carries a powerful implication for your memorization journey, as well as passing the gift onto somebody else! **"In all things, I have shown you that by working hard in this way we must help**

the weak and remember the words of the Lord Jesus, how he himself said, 'It is more blessed to give than to receive.'" Acts 20:35 (ESV).

God blessed me with the ability to teach people the practice of Hope in Numbers for years and see the harvests grow in their lives. There are many different ways to introduce people to Hope in Numbers, and in this chapter, I will share some of the best practices.

Sharing Best Practices

Before I get into some ways that I share Hope in Numbers with other people, I want to make a few things clear. Throughout this book, I have shared my personal experiences with Hope in Numbers and how I memorize scripture. God made us all unique individuals, and we may also be unique in how we best memorize scripture or teach it to others. Therefore, I pray we can become a community of Hope in Numbers ambassadors who learn personal best practices and then share those best practices with anyone who needs help learning how to do this or how to teach someone else.

I'm inviting you to join our community where we sharpen each other, like iron sharpens iron, by sharing our best practices and encouraging one another. Whenever you have a best practice to share, a Hope in Numbers story, or an insightful way to teach someone else this practice, please make a video or a photo and share it on any social media platform with the hashtag #HopeInNumbersBestPractices.

Social media can impact and engage people with the gospel and encourage them to memorize His Word through numbers. I believe in the power of community and using social media as a tool for evangelism and sharing the hope of the world, Jesus Christ! As believers, we must understand that we have the greatest

Chapter 5 - Teach it

news that the world is desperate to hear! The gospel can heal, redeem and save souls for eternity. **"For I am not ashamed of the gospel, for it is the power of God for salvation to everyone who believes, to the Jew first and also to the Greek"** Romans 1:16 (ESV).

We should be bold in wanting to share and teach others God's Word through numbers. If the Bible is true and has the power to change somebody's life for the better, then why should we hesitate? Let's press forward and wreck this world for Jesus Christ! Would you like to join me in starting a revolution of Bible-believing saints who are unashamed to share the Gospel of Jesus Christ? Then follow me as I follow Him!

In reality, you might be the only Christian that somebody else knows, and God wants you to step up to the plate and take a swing for their eternity. God can make seeds grow, but God needs someone to plant them for Him. You will have many opportunities to plant seeds by practicing these five steps of Holding Onto Promises Everywhere. Any time you are with somebody, you can bet you will pass by a number. Will you take advantage of the opportunity and share with that person for what they are desperate? It is my prayer that you will share hope with them! I will give you some tools and strategies that have worked for me, as well as the confidence to follow through. **"So do not throw away your confidence; it will be richly rewarded"** Hebrews 10:35 (NIV).

Give People Their Birthday Bible Verse

The easiest and most effective way to share with somebody a timely Bible verse and the idea of Hope in Numbers is by showing them their Birthday Bible Verse. Most people have not heard before that the date of their birth can have a promise from God attached. The verse usually has a strong connection with

125

that person. Some even remember it right on the spot. How cool is that?

I can't express people's excitement when I walk around and ask others for their birthday and give them their Birthday Bible Verse on the spot. I do this not to impress people but bless people with the coolest way to memorize God's Word and hold it close to them everywhere they go. You are holding in your hand a book with every Birthday Bible Verse in the back, so you can go around with this book and bless others while introducing them to this new idea of finding true Hope in Numbers through their birthday!

Hope Walks & Drives

Another great way to share the power of seeing Hope in Numbers with people and teaching them to see it is by going on what I call Hope Walks and Drives. It can be a stroll to the park, around the block, or the mall as you speak life into somebody. Hope Walks is something I do in my quiet time with God, but it is also a very non-threatening way to introduce somebody to God's Word. When you share Hope in Numbers with someone on a walk, most people will think it's pretty cool that you saw a number and memorized a scripture that went along with it. Some will think it's so cool that they will want to try it! That, my friends, is the goal! **"And he said to them, 'Follow me, and I will make you fishers of men'"** Matthew 4:19 (ESV).

Not only does Hope Walks work well for alone time with God and evangelism with others, but Hope Drives work wonders, too! Just think about it. When you are in the car by yourself or with somebody else, there are numbers everywhere. Street signs, license plates, gas prices, freeway exit signs, and more! It's the perfect opportunity for a verse to come up that you have already memorized to mesmerize somebody else and get them excited about knowing God's Word by heart! You can easily explain to them the benefits of Holding Onto Promises Everywhere and BOOM! You are fishing for men, just like Jesus said!

There are so many treasure boxes around us to share God's Word because numbers are everywhere we look, and you now have the key to unlock the box! The time of day, the date on the calendar, and the temperature outside are just a few quick examples. What if you see an awesome, timely Bible verse out in the world, but you aren't around anybody to share it? Well, you know that fantastic piece of technology sitting in your pocket? The great thing about the world we live in is we can use our smartphones and connect with friends, family, and acquaintances whenever we want! You can record a quick video or snap a photo to share your timely Bible verse with somebody or everybody you know so that they can be blessed by your Hope in Numbers find!

I try to do this as much as I can, and I get comments about how the particular story and verse have blessed their life. You can do this too! I always get a kick out of how God uses situations in my life as an opportunity to share Hope in Numbers with not only the people around me, but also with others on social media. I want to tell you about a few #HashtagMoments that gave me an open door to share Jesus through Hope in Numbers!

#Hashtag Moments for Jesus
In the last year, while writing this book, I found myself in many different situations where I was able to share and teach this gift to random people. I call it #HashtagMomentsForJesus because these God moments were way too cool not to share them on social media! Some situations felt like unfortunate incidents, while others were seemingly good in their entirety. God used all of them to bless others by using this gift! Here are some examples of how all situations can be an opportunity for you to bless others!

Hope in Numbers

    Recently, I needed to schedule an appointment with the dentist to get two root canals done. Not a pleasant thought-having surgery on your teeth, but it ended up being a great time! Here's why. While the dentist worked on my teeth, he asked me what all the numbers represented on my Hope in Numbers bracelet. So, with that opportunity, I shared with him all of the verses and how you can see a Bible verse in any number you see!

    I blew his mind. Minutes later, his receptionist came to me and wanted to know more about it and what church I attended. So, I told her and asked if she ever personally asked Jesus into her heart. She said no, but she really wanted to go to church! I gave her this verse in Romans 10:9 (NIV): **"If you declare with your mouth, 'Jesus is Lord,' and believe in your heart that God raised him from the dead, you will be saved."** I told her if she prays this Bible verse and truly believes it, she will be saved! On-the-spot evangelism through Hope in Numbers!

    This was the first of many #HashtagMomentsForJesus stories I've recently had. I was there to get my teeth fixed, but truthfully God allowed me to fix someone else's spirit on Jesus, and we enjoyed every minute of talking about Hope in Numbers. #RootCanalsForJesus

    In the last few months, while writing this book, I've gotten four flat tires total: three on my vehicle and one on my wife's. With the last one I got, my wife started laughing at me, knowing how much the devil's been coming after me with distractions from writing this book. I dread car problems more than anything else because I'm not mechanically inclined. I tell people it's not my gift, but wrecking lives for Jesus is! Since I became a frequent customer at Discount Tire, I became friends with a guy there and shared his Birthday Bible verse with him on August 31st (8/31). Romans 8:31 (NIV) says, **"What, then, shall we say in response to these things? If God is for us, who can be against us?"** #FlatTiresForJesus

Chapter 5 - Teach it

Within that same period of getting the flat tires, one of my van windows broke in the middle of a hot Arizona summer. It was 112 degrees outside. James 1:12 (NIV) says, **"Blessed is the one who perseveres under trial because, having stood the test, that person will receive the crown of life that the Lord has promised to those who love him."** The repair man came to my house to fix it. I was able to bring up Hope in Numbers to him through the weather and his birthday. The guy started following me immediately on social media! #BrokenWindowsForJesus

One morning after staying up late getting a lot of this book written, I was driving to work down Interstate 17 in Phoenix when a piece of debris flew out of someone's work truck and struck the front of my van. It caused an estimated $4,000 in damage and repairs and took over a month and a half to get fixed. The repair shop that I went to was owned by a man who was a Christian, and naturally, I shared with him his Birthday Bible verse, and he was blessed by it! His birthday was July 7th (7/17), and the associated scripture was Psalms 71:7 (NLT) **"My life is an example to many, because you have my strength and protection."** BOOM! #FreewayCollisionsForJesus

Here's one last example of a seemingly bad situation that God turned around as an opportunity to bless somebody with the hope they needed! Every year at my work, they ask us to take a health evaluation to save money on our health insurance. If you give blood, you can lower your rate for health insurance. I always decide to do it because I'm all about saving money and staying debt-free, thanks to the Dave Ramsey Plan, which I love! Although I am a diabetic and I give myself shots all the time, the one thing I dread is giving blood. It's one of the worst experiences for me.

Anyways, my wife forced me to give blood, and a few days later, the health evaluation team called me, and I panicked. I thought they would tell me I had some fatal disease or something. Luckily, they weren't calling me for that reason, but they were calling to tell me that I needed to get my blood redrawn because they had lost my previous sample! I thought, are you kidding me?

So, I went back to get blood drawn for a second time in one week because I knew Dave Ramsey would be upset with me if he found out I didn't take the opportunity to save money! This time, when I went, I overheard the people drawing blood and talking about Jesus. I started to get excited inside because I knew I was about to share with them Hope in Numbers! So, when the opportunity came, I shared the ministry and told them their Birthday Bible verses, and they loved it! This verse came to my mind as I gave blood: **"And they defeated him by the blood of the Lamb and by their testimony"** Revelations 12:11 (NLT). #GettingBloodDrawnForJesus

Those were some of the unfortunate moments when God allowed me to share the gift of Hope in Numbers. Now, looking back, I'm grateful for those moments. They would have never been possible without something first going wrong. Gave has been giving me a perspective to embrace every moment!

It doesn't have to happen that way. Sharing Hope in Numbers is possible at any time, in any place, and with anyone! Good times also give plenty of opportunities to teach somebody else the power of seeing God's Word in numbers. Here are a few examples of some experiences I've had.

I was at the AT&T store with my brother Russ asking questions about the new iPhone and ignited hope in the employee's heart who was serving us through a quick Hope in Numbers demonstration. There have been times when everyone at the barber shop asks me their Birthday Bible verse. I'm telling you—teaching this to people is fun and contagious! People catch the fire quickly. I've used Hope in Numbers to start random conversations with people in lines at stores, in the streets, and at work! It's a cool way to evangelize.

Once a police officer stopped me and asked me what I was doing in the parking lot by other people's cars making videos. I had to tell him about what I was doing and seeing Hope in Numbers on people's license plates. I quoted a few verses to the police officer, and he was cool with what I was doing! Even the Discover Card security guard thought I was breaking into people's cars once, and I had to explain to him that I was quoting Bible verses. #AlmostGettingArrestedForJesus

I've even taught my best friend to start teaching and showing other people this gift. He made a video once of going through the McDonald's drive-thru and asking the guy at the cash register what the total bill was. The guy said "$4.13." My friend quoted Philippians 4:13 (NLT): **"I can do all things through Christ who gives me strength."** And the guy didn't know what hit him! Who knows what that planted seed might become? #DriveThroughsForJesus

Last, quick story for you! On our anniversary, my wife, Cindy, and I went to Olive Garden, and the bill was $24.11, and I thought, this is perfect! I'll make the tip $5 to total $29.11 and put "Jeremiah" on it. I told her to look up this Bible verse for the bill. Jeremiah 29:11 (NIV) says, **"For I know the plans I have for you," declares the Lord, "plans to prosper you and not to harm you, plans to give you hope and a future."** #LeaveTipsForJesus

Do you see how fun and easy it can be to share God's Word with someone? Even strangers who don't even know you can be blessed through your help to see and hear God's Word in a fun, new way! You can start teaching the world to see Hope in Numbers today!

A Gym for Your Soul

In today's world, people spend tons of money on their fitness. They purchase monthly gym memberships, home workout equipment, nutrition plans, and even hire personal trainers. That is all good and worthy, but here is what the Bible says **"For physical training is of some value, but godliness has value for all things, holding promise for both the present life and the life to come"** 1 Timothy 4:8 (NIV). So, God's Word says that godliness is more valuable than physical fitness. Why wouldn't we spend as much time and energy to gain godliness and spiritual fitness?

With that said, you can work to become physically fit by lifting weights at a gym, but you can become a person of great spiritual fitness by practicing Hope in Numbers! You will become joyful in the Lord when you know His Word by heart and can recite scripture on the spot! When you know how to exercise your faith muscles through Hope in Numbers, you can also become a trainer to help others get spiritually fit! You will, metaphorically, have a spiritual six-pack that other people will want to have themselves! Trust me, I have people often telling me they wish they could do what I do, and I tell them that they can! Start today, start small, and the results will come!

Hope in Numbers will help you lose some unwanted spiritual weight on your soul. Hebrews 12:1 (NLT) says, **"Therefore, since we are surrounded by such a huge crowd of witnesses to the life of faith, let us strip off every weight that slows us down, especially the sin that so easily trips us up. And let us run with endurance the race God has set before us."** Why not become spiritually fit this year and take on the battles that are not of flesh and blood but of spirit? It will be beneficial and valuable for all things!

Chapter 5 - Teach it

Spiritual Six-Pack Challenge

What are the six areas in your life that you need to work out and get stronger in? With the help of God's Word, you can strategically find six Bible verses that will help you in areas where you are weak. Memorize them and apply them to your life with Hope in Numbers so you can reign victorious! **"No, in all these things we are more than conquerors through him who loved us"** Romans 8:37 (NIV).

Fill in the six blanks with the areas where you struggle. Here are some examples: Anger, lust, fear, worry, doubt, swearing, drinking, and gossip. The quickest way to find Bible verses about the areas in life you struggle with is by opening up the YouVersion Bible app on your phone and searching the topic in the search function. It will pull up all the verses that have that particular word. Pick the verse you like most to help you and write it below.

Bible Verse - _____
_____
_____
_____
_____

Bible Verse - _____
_____
_____
_____
_____

Bible Verse - _____
_____
_____
_____
_____

Hope in Numbers

Bible Verse - _____
_____
_____
_____
_____

Bible Verse - _____
_____
_____
_____
_____

Bible Verse - _____
_____
_____
_____
_____

Gym for Your Soul Activity

The biggest key to getting into shape physically, mentally, or spiritually is having a routine and staying consistent. With consistency comes confidence. Confidence will give you the courage to keep moving forward. There is so much power in having a consistent routine and forming good habits. Just like when someone is serious about working out, they set a routine and plan their workouts: some days of the week are dedicated leg workouts, and others are for the chest, back, or core.

    I want to challenge you to get out of your comfort zone and start a spiritual workout plan that will push you into a weekly routine that will help you grow into the best spiritual fitness of your life! It is a simple plan that produces confident, Christ-centered difference makers, which God calls us to be! Check out an example of what a weekly "gym for your soul" looks like:

Chapter 5 - Teach it

<u>Monday</u> - Praise Day - Psalms 92:1
Lord, it is good to praise you. Most High God, it is good to make music to honor you.

On this day, I want you to dedicate time alone to be with God and worship him through song. It could be on a car ride or during your quiet time. Just at some point during the day, get into the presence of the Lord through worship music.

Some of my favorites worship bands you should look up are: Elevation worship, Hillsong United Worship, Bethel Music, Chris Tomlin, Casting Crowns, Mercy Me, Crowder Band, Matthew West, Jeremy Camp, Sidewalk Prophets, Lauren Daigle, CCV Music, Passion, Vineyard Worship and Lecrae.

<u>Tuesday</u> - Leg Day - James 2:18
Now someone may argue, "Some people have faith; others have good deeds." But I say, "How can you show me your faith if you don't have good deeds? I will show you my faith by my good deeds."

On this day, be the hands and feet of Jesus to someone in need. Help meet their physical or spiritual needs. "**Let us think of ways to motivate one another to acts of love and good works**" Hebrews 10:24 (NLT).

<u>Wednesday</u> - Core/Foundation day - Ephesians 2:20
You are built on the foundation of the apostles and prophets, with King Jesus himself as the cornerstone.

On this day, watch a Bible teaching from one of your favorite pastors that you can find on YouTube, a podcast, or their church app.

<u>Thursday</u> - Pull Up Day - 1 Thessalonians 5:11
So, encourage each other and build each other up, just as you are already doing.

Hope in Numbers

<u>On this day, build someone up with your words and actions. Each week pick someone different, speak life into that person, and watch as it refreshes you too.</u>

<u>Friday</u> - Prayer Day - James 5:16

Confess your sins to each other and pray for each other so that you may be healed. The earnest prayer of a righteous person has great power and produces wonderful results.

On this day, dedicate some time to praying for friends and family. Text the person and let them know you're praying for them. It will encourage them. Watch God start to answer prayers for you, your friends, and your family.

<u>Saturday</u> - Serve Day - Mark 10:45

For even the Son of Man came not to be served but to serve others and to give his life as a ransom for many.

On this day, find a place to serve your neighbor, community, or church. You could likely help your neighbors and communities likely with yard work. I know many churches have Saturday church service, where you could help serve. **"Never let the fire in your heart go out. Keep it alive. Serve The Lord"** Romans 12:11 (NIRV).

<u>Sunday</u> - Recovery Day - Exodus 20:8-10

Remember to observe the Sabbath day by keeping it holy. You have six days each week for your ordinary work, but the seventh day is a Sabbath day of rest dedicated to the Lord your God. On that day no one in your household may do any work.

On this day, relax. Take the day off and refuel spiritually. Remember, God created the world in six days, and on the seventh day, He rested. Not because He was tired but because He wanted

Chapter 5 - Teach it

to be an example of how to live the most successful life. God created the world in six days. Can you imagine what He could do in your life if you would take on this challenge every week and let God work through you?

Imagine the results a weekly spiritual fitness plan like this can have on your life. Take some time to develop your spiritual fitness plan. It will take some discipline to get started initially, but you will feel so alive spiritually that it will be worth every ounce of discipline. Let's see what mountains God can move through you!

Hear a testimony from a brother in Christ about how practicing Hope in Numbers gave him a new sense of confidence in the Word of God!

My name Is JoeJoe, and I live in the state of California. I want to take a moment to share with you how Hope in Numbers changed my life. I was going through a really tough period at the beginning of 2017. I was struggling immensely with my faith in the pit. Out of nowhere, I received a message alert on my phone and noticed that Gordon was on a live video. I had no idea who this guy was, but I felt a nudge in my heart and couldn't turn off this video. As he demonstrated his powerful gift from God in Hope in Numbers, I thought it was fascinating! Then, he took a step further and personally asked me what my birthday was so he could give me my Birthday Verse.

Now Gordon has been teaching me how to use Hope in Numbers and memorize verses that connect with specific numbers. Hope in Numbers has changed my life because I am now able to speak the Bible into existence in my life.

Now my relationships have been restored. My wife, Cassandra, and I just got married on 7.9.2017; the Hope in Numbers for that date is "If you do not stand firm in your faith, you will not stand at all" (Isaiah 7:9 NLT). That is now one of my favorite promises from the Lord to keep me focused on my faith.

Thank you, Gordon, for sharing the gift the Lord has blessed you with! Now, I can also share this gift of Hope in Numbers with everyone around me.

Daily Fire

As part of my ministry, I send out a daily encouragement text message to over one hundred people who have asked me for a Hope in Numbers verse of the day with a coordinating image. Back in the day, my teachers in school would say: *an apple a day keeps the doctor away*, but Jesus told me: *a Bible verse a day keeps the devil away!*

People are shocked that I personally send each person a separate text message and not a massive group text. I do this because I want people to respond, and I do not want others to be annoyed by a big group message. I want to be able to minister to each person individually and message them back and forth if they'd like to. **"But encourage one another daily, as long as it is called 'Today,' so that none of you may be hardened by sin's deceitfulness"** Hebrews 3:13 (NIV). I also do it because it helps me to fulfill this step of teaching Hope in Numbers to others. They can also pass these images and verses to their friends and family!

I feel this verse come alive in my life when I send out the daily fire: **"The generous will prosper; those who refresh others will themselves be refreshed"** Proverbs 11:25 (NLT). I always feel great after sending these out every day. Like Pastor Brian Houston once said, "Encouragement is an investment into someone else's future." I believe that to be true. That is why I am a big fan of encouraging others.

I encourage you to go to any of the Hope in Numbers' social media pages, save the daily Bible verse image or other encouraging photos, and start your own daily fire by sharing them with your friends and family. It doesn't take that long, and you can start small, maybe five people? Watch and see if it grows from there. Can you imagine if everyone who reads this book did this? God's Word would spread like wildfire!

The Righteous Pyramid Scheme for Jesus

I'm in the business of taking things of this world back for Jesus Christ and turning seemingly "worldly" terms back to the powerful message of Christ! One of the terms that many business opportunity people hear is a term called a pyramid scheme. A pyramid scheme is an illegal business practice based on people recruiting people only without selling a legitimate service or product- the person at the top of the organization gets paid most of the money for the business. That's the best way I can explain a pyramid scheme.

You can think of Hope in Numbers as a righteous pyramid scheme for team Jesus Christ and the church. What we sell is blessings and righteousness through faith in God's Word! **"And the word of God increased; and the number of the disciples multiplied in Jerusalem exceedingly; and a great company of the priests were obedient to the faith"** Acts 6:7 (ASV). The world may not think believe we have a legitimate product, but we know the Word of God has the power to save souls for eternity!

As Hope in Numbers ambassadors, we fall under Jesus Christ and His twelve disciples who started the church. We profit through stronger faith and encouragement from one another— **"that is, that you and I may be mutually encouraged by each other's faith"** Romans 1:12 (NIV). Hope in Numbers is a great way to bless others, get them excited about the Lord, and motivate them to join Team Jesus and His church!

Think about it. Jesus changed the face of this planet through twelve disciples that He trained. He sent them to make disciples until one day, **"at the name of Jesus every knee should bow, in heaven and on earth and under the earth, and every**

tongue confess that Jesus Christ is Lord, the glory of God the Father" Philippians 2:10-11 (NKJV). Now that's the power of the righteous pyramid scheme—training others in the Word of God and proclaiming the Truth of the Gospel!

I've made this process as simple as possible to build this pyramid for Jesus by having five steps to follow. You can help others discover God's promises out in the world and hold them in their hearts forever. We can fulfill the great commission and help grow God's Kingdom by holding onto promises everywhere we go and teaching them this T.R.U.T.H. process. **"Therefore go and make disciples of all nations, baptizing them in the name of the Father and of the Son and of the Holy Spirit, and teaching them to obey everything I have commanded you. And surely I am with you always, to the very end of the age"** Matthew 28:19-20 (NLT).

The Righteous Pyramid Challenge

Are you willing to contribute to the building of God's Kingdom and tell others about the love of God and the free gift of grace through Jesus Christ? It all starts with sharing with someone the truth and wisdom from God's Word.

If you are willing, commit right now to telling five people about God's Word through Hope in Numbers. Write their names below, and check the box to the left when you've accomplished your goal.

Names
1._____
2._____
3._____
4._____
5._____

CHAPTER 6 - HOLD IT

Moving onto the fifth and final step of the Hope in Numbers T.R.U.T.H process, I am sharing what it means to "HOLD IT". It's the last step of the process, and once you have all five steps working together, it will be as if you are holding onto your hope with all five of your fingers for maximum grip! Without all five of your fingers holding onto hope, your hope can get ripped away by the evil one. But once you are working all five steps and have your full grasp on this process, you can take back your hope into your possession by ripping it out from the hand of the enemy! This is what it means to Hold Onto Promises Everywhere and follow the T.R.U.T.H.: **"To the Jews who had believed him, Jesus said, 'If you hold to my teaching, you are really my**

disciples. Then you will know the truth, and the truth will set you free.'" John 8:31-32 (NIV).

Hope is in every number. You can now take hold of it because you know this process. The world and the evil one will try to discourage you and distract you from using this gift, but don't let that happen! Rip your hope out of the devil's hand and keep it secure and safe in your hand by keeping God's Word close to your heart!

No matter how small of progress you are making, I will give you this advice: Do not give up! This process will get easier and easier as you continue to practice it. **"Let us not become weary in doing good, for at the proper time we will reap a harvest if we do not give up"** Galatians 6:9 (NIV). Hold onto the little progress that you make and watch as God starts to bless your perspective. **"But we must hold on to the progress we have already made"** Philippians 3:16 (NLT).

Congratulate yourself for reading the book until this point! You decided to continue even when it was long or became difficult! It tells me you dedicate yourself to practicing your faith in this new way and are willing to give Hope in Numbers a real shot! For that, I celebrate with you! Holding onto your hope in God's Word is a lot like marriage. It's wonderful to be in love, and quiting is not an option when times get tough.

Holding Onto My Marriage

I am now a happily married man to my beautiful wife, Cindy, whom I met at Discover Card. The two blessings I discovered at Discover Card were the gift of Hope in Numbers and my one-of-a-kind wife, Cindy. She was my supervisor when we first started seeing each other. So, once news broke that we were going to church together, they made us switch teams. We like to say we found love in a hopeless place!

Chapter 6 - Hold It

After going through a divorce and never wanting to go through that again, I did some serious soul-searching and promised God that I would never go without seeking Him first in everything I do. I made a promise like this in my first marriage and failed. I felt like the apostle Peter felt moments before Jesus was crucified when he said to Him, "I would never leave you, Jesus!" and then moments later denied knowing Him.

So, after my divorce, when Jesus resurrected my life, I committed to Him that I would never deny Him again! He would be the center of my life for the rest of my life. Until I die, I will lift Jesus' name high, just like Peter eventually did, even to the point of death.

Therefore, before I asked Cindy to marry me, I went to the light pole at work with the number 15, where I would kneel in prayer like Tim Tebow and asked, "God, should I marry Cindy? God, please give me a sign." The second I stood up from kneeling, a car drove by with a pink CCV sticker, and it became my sign for "Go!"

CCV is the church Cindy and I started attending full-time, and we decided to make it our home church around this time! My mind was blown. I knew it was confirmation that I should marry Cindy. I believe God answered my prayer within seconds. Again, I didn't believe it was a coincidence, but evidence from God that I should move forward and marry her.

Hope in Numbers was just starting at this time in my life. So, I started brainstorming cool ways to use Hope in Numbers for my proposal to her. I felt the Lord prompting me to ask her to marry me on May 12th (5/12) because that day was a very special day for me back in 2008 when the doctor said my son, Andrew, went from death to life. Remember, when he was born, the doctors had said he had zero chance to live, but on May 12, 2008, his chances went to sixty percent chance to live!

Hope in Numbers

Since, metaphorically, I was coming back from death to life from my first marriage, I figured this was a perfect day to ask Cindy to marry me and to start a new life together! The Hope in Numbers verse for that day comes from Psalms 5:12 (NLT): **"For you bless the godly, O Lord; you surround them with your shield of love."** Looking back over the past five years of our marriage, that's what the Lord has done for us! He has blessed and surrounded us with a shield of love that I can't even fathom. I can't make this up. While writing this part in the book, our little three-year-old daughter, Hope, walked into my office and gave me a big hug out of nowhere! Jesus has blessed us!

So, not only did I pick a fire Hope In Numbers date on the calendar to ask Cindy to marry me, but I also knew exactly where and when I wanted to ask her to marry me. At our church, there's a small mountain on campus with a full-sized cross at the peak of it. I knew for sure I wanted to propose to Cindy at the foot of the cross at 6:33 a.m. because I knew this marriage needed to be built on the promise from God in Matthew 6:33 (NIV): **"But seek first his kingdom and his righteousness, and all these things will be given to you as well."**

The night before my planned proposal, I asked her daughter, Calista, if I could marry her mom as her dad was no longer in the picture. Ky said, "Yes, of course, you can marry my mom." The next day, I asked Cindy to hike to the top of the CCV mountain to get a cross and sunrise picture with me. I set my alarm to go off at 6:30 a.m. so I would be ready to pop the question at exactly 6:33 a.m.

When the time finally came, I got on one knee and asked her to marry me at exactly 6:33 a.m. she said YES! I told her that as long as, in our marriage, we keep Jesus first, the Lord will bless it. That promise from Matthew is one hundred percent true and continues to bless us to this day. After the proposal, I took

Chapter 6 - Hold It

Cindy across the street to this fine hamburger restaurant called McDonald's. My pastor, Craig Beyer, once told me if you want to see if a girl really likes you, then take her to a low-quality restaurant during a really special time and see if she still likes you afterward. That's what I did, and it went well!

The wildest thing happened as we walked out of McDonald's that morning. The first license plate we saw in the parking lot had the number 633 on it, and I have the picture to prove it! Matthew 6:33 was the Bible verse that started Hope in Numbers, and now it started my marriage in the right direction.

The marriage planning was on, and my soon-to-be wife came up with the coolest idea to use our wedding as an avenue for witnessing to all our friends and family who might not yet be believers in Christ. We decided to get married on August 31st (8/31, it became another foundational marriage scripture we would build our marriage. Romans 8:31 (NIV) says, **"If God is for us, who can be against us?"** Having a marriage scripture is crucial; it gives you a firm promise to hold on to when times are tough!

We planned for our marriage ceremony to be on the top of the same mountain I proposed on. We would get married at the foot of the cross. We had nearly one hundred people climb to attend our ceremony at the top of the mountain. Afterward, we had everybody from the ceremony attend the regular church service so those who did not attend church regularly could hear the good news of Jesus!

After service, we had our friends and family eat in our church's amazing cafe. We planned our whole wedding around having our non-believing friends and family witness a life-changing church evening. We tricked them into coming to church, and it was a beautiful night!

Making Vows

One thing that my marriage has taught me about holding onto love comes from scripture—**"Don't just pretend to love others. Really love them. Hate what is wrong. Hold tightly to what is good"** Romans 12:9 (NLT). I see goodness in my wife, and I love and hold onto her for that reason. This same concept is true for the Lord! I hold tightly onto His Word over everything else because I have experienced the goodness and favor of the Lord! **"We love because he first loved us"** 1 John 4:19 (NIV). When you apply God's Word in your life, you too will understand how much God loves you, cares for you, and gave up His Son to start an eternal relationship with you.

That is the reason Jesus came down to earth to die for us. He wanted us to commit our lives to follow Him. Jesus wants to marry His church and be with His people forever. In the Bible, Jesus compares himself to a husband and the church to a wife.

"Husbands, love your wives, as Christ loved the church and gave himself up for her, that he might sanctify her, having cleansed her by the washing of water with the word, so that he might present the church to himself in splendor, without spot or wrinkle or any such thing, that she might be holy and without blemish" Ephesians 5:25-27 (ESV). God is so good and has proven His love for us by sending His one and only Son to die for us on the cross. Now that is redemption!

In most wedding vows, you will hear something like this: "In the name of God, I, Gordon, take you, Cindy, to be my wife. To have and hold from this day forward, for better, for worse, for richer, for poorer, in sickness and health, to love and cherish, until death do we part. This is my solemn vow." As Christians, we can pretty much make and declare a similar vow to the Lord: "In the name of God, I, Gordon, take you, Jesus, to be the Lord of my life, to have and to hold you from this day forward, for better, for worse, for richer, for poorer, in sickness and in health, to love and to seek you first, until the day I die. This is my solemn vow."

The amazing reality is Jesus already declared this vow to you when He died on the cross and rose again. The Creator of the universe is freely offering you the gift of grace, no condemnation, and undeserved righteousness. How amazing is that? Jesus wants you to know His love personally and to say "Yes!" to Him. Have you accepted His invitation to commit yourself to follow Jesus and His Word for the rest of your life? **"Every word of God is flawless; he is a shield to those who take refuge in him"** Proverbs 30:5 (NIV).

If you would like to make this vow to Jesus right now, write your name in the blank below. Then write down the date and the Hope in Numbers for this day you make this vow to Him. Also, if you are already a follower of Jesus, you can renew your vow to Him.

Hope in Numbers

"If you declare with your mouth, 'Jesus is Lord,' and believe in your heart that God raised him from the dead, you will be saved" Romans 10:9 (NIV)

"In the name of God, I, _____, take you, Jesus, to be the Lord of my life, to have and hold from this day forward, for better, for worse, for richer, for poorer, in sickness and health, to love and seek you first, until the day I die. This is my solemn vow.

Date:_____
The Bible verse date this commitment was signed on:
_____
_____
_____
_____
_____
_____

Congratulations! If you signed this commitment, declared it with your mouth, and believed it in your heart, then welcome to the family of the Lord! You've made the best decision of your life!

"So, God has given both his promise and his oath. These two things are unchangeable because it is impossible for God to lie. Therefore, we who have fled to him for refuge can have great confidence as we hold to the hope that lies before us" Hebrews 6:18 (NLT).

Choosing A Retirement Verse

Since we are talking about marriage and choosing to follow Jesus for the rest of our lives, it is only fitting to now move into talks of retirement and choosing a verse that you will invest in for the

Chapter 6 - Hold It

rest of your life! In marriage or life, people work all their lives and invest their hard-earned money into a retirement fund. I think it is paramount that we also choose a verse to say, "This is a verse that I live by and invest my life in!"

My retirement verse is Matthew 6:33 (ESV): **"But seek first the kingdom of God and his righteousness, and all these things will be added to you."** I have it sewn on my hats and make it my goal to live it out daily. The power of having a verse you dedicate your life to is that you can return to it if you stumble or fall, and it will point you back in the best direction for your life.

I want to challenge you to pick a verse that you can bank on. A scripture you dedicate your life to and put your spiritual investment in it. Don't rush this process but follow through and pick one!

Write down your retirement verse here: _____
_____
_____
_____
_____
_____
_____
_____

Possess God's Word

As a follower of Jesus and an active user of the gift of Hope in Numbers, you are partaking in a lifelong journey and never-ending discovery of the majesties of our Lord Jesus Christ. God's sovereign ways will always bring you a fresh revelation of His Word and tie them together with numbers to create awesome Hope in Numbers stories. As you start memorizing more Bible verses and have a memory bank full of His promises, remember always to have a humble heart. Again, we don't use this gift to impress others but to bless them. In essence, we want to possess God's Word, not just be professors of it.

In the times of Jesus, there were religious leaders called Pharisees who grew up learning scripture and memorizing it word by word, like what I teach. Here's the difference between the teachings. When the Lord Jesus was in the presence of the Pharisees, they hated Jesus and looked for ways to kill him. How could this be? These people studied God's Word and even had it memorized but could not bear to be in the presence of God in the flesh. Although these Jewish professors had God's Word firmly planted in their heads, they did not allow the Word to consume their hearts and change them from the inside out.

To be a full possessor of God's Word, we must hold the promises not just planted in our minds but firmly in our hearts. As we meditate and use God's Word for its divine purpose, we will get a clear revelation of the person of Jesus, and that revelation changes everything. Jesus is in the business of transforming hearts. When we let Him do that, He is sure to deliver. Let us learn to make it a habit to hold onto this T.R.U.T.H. and possess His Word in our hearts. Let it transform who we are as people of God. **"So, get rid of all the filth and evil in your lives, and humbly accept the word God has planted in your hearts, for it has the power to save your souls"** James 1:21 (NLT).

Hold It Til It's A Habit

Habits are a part of humanity. We all form them, whether good or bad. If I get out of my daily habits, it throws my day completely off track. For example, every day, I bring a bag of Dill Pickle Sunflower Seeds and a two-liter bottle of Diet Mountain Dew to drink and snack on at work. If I forget to bring them with me,

Chapter 6 - Hold It

I feel terrible. My attitude that day is not as pleasing. Therefore, I make sure to plan ahead and not forget those two things. The same happens if I forget my headphones or iPhone because the Lord knows I need those to listen to worship music and sermon messages.

The same thing happens to my day if I get out of my daily habit of seeing Hope in Numbers. My spiritual conviction gets flipped, I get easily distracted, and temptations start coming at me. I'm careful to keep my daily habits in order, so I stay steadfast in the Lord and remain in His presence. One great piece of advice I learned from my pastor is that we shouldn't make the number of Bible verses we have memorized the goal or reward, but instead, make the daily habit the goal and reward! Again, it's not about an end goal of saying I have this number of verses memorized. Your desire will fade away with that as your goal. Instead, look to the activity and opportunity to memorize verses as your goal and reward.

Remember, my son Andrew would love the opportunity to memorize Bible verses. Unfortunately, he is not able to, but you are! Please, make it your reward to do this daily because it truly is a blessing!

Hope in Numbers is just like anything else that is worthwhile in life. It might be hard at first, but when you continue in it, it becomes a habit. Remember the first time you typed on a keyboard and how slowly it took to type out a paragraph? Now, you can type quickly without looking or thinking about it. That is why you practice, and practice, something like Hope in Numbers until it becomes a habit!

Once this practice becomes a habit, you will collect a memory bank of treasure from above that will bless your life in so many ways! Unlike many other things, it is okay to hoard God's Word and keep it in your heart!

Hoard It

The Truth is God's Word has life-changing benefits. His word is life to the dead and health to the sick. He is light to those living in darkness and freedom to those living in bondage. God wants you to know His word, live it abundantly, and even hoard it in your heart. The definition of "hoard" is to accumulate for preservation and future use in a hidden or carefully guarded place. Hoarding God's Word in your heart will give your spirit fullness and ammo you have not known before. Your spirit will be a bank account of spiritual blessings ready to give back to you at times of need and to others who need it most.

The world knows the word "hoard" as something negative where a person is obsessive about keeping material items in their homes, garages, or basements for safekeeping. A TV show called "Hoarders" shows how delirious people can get when they hoard physical items in their homes and do not throw anything away. But in the spiritual world in which we live, it is very beneficial to hoard God's Word to keep us from sin so we can live our best life. **"I have stored up your word in my heart, that I might not sin against you"** Psalm 119:11 (ESV).

All Christians should hoard God's Word in their hearts for when life's circumstances come their way and the enemy is trying to defeat them. Unfortunately for the devil, he is no match for God's Word. Other people are losing the battle of their faith because they lack spiritual ammunition, but when you become a storehouse of God's treasures, you will be well-equipped to supply a timely Word of faith to keep you safe.

What a blessing you can be to others if you hoard God's Word in your heart! Take advantage of this blessing. Not everybody in the world gets to hold a Bible in their hands without being persecuted for it. Let us represent the Light of this world by holding onto His Word, making it a habit, and hoarding as much of it as we can!

Texas Hold'em

As I was writing this "Hold It" chapter, I felt God tugging on my heart to share with you a scarred wound from my past. God has been faithful in using my past hurts and pain for His glory and gain. I relate with Paul when he humbly said, **"Even if I am to be poured out as a drink offering upon the sacrificial offering of your faith, I am glad and rejoice with you all"** Philippians 2:17 (ESV). I share this story with you because it testifies to how God rescued me from the pit of addiction. I hope to shed some light on helpful ways to encourage others who have destructive habits to break the chains of addiction with the help of Jesus!

My high school friends and I started gambling with the game Texas Hold'em. At first, it was just innocent fun with friends, playing with pocket change. Yet, over a few years, when we started to get real jobs, a few dollars in the pot turned into hundreds of dollars. Isn't that exactly how sin works in our lives too? It starts small and seemingly innocent, but then it continues to grow and grow until one day, it becomes a massive issue in your life, and you can't stop using your own.

Honestly, gambling in high school became a stronghold and destructive addiction. I lost lots of money, and my friends were getting into fights; it was terrible! That kind of gambling is never good! I couldn't stop gambling with my own willpower; I needed help from a higher power, and that higher power was the love of Jesus Christ! When I became a Christian on December 7, 2001 (12/7/2001), I put down the playing cards and pursued Jesus instead. It was a great feeling to finally be free from the chains of a gambling addiction!

I thought I was completely free from the power of this destructive habit forever, but one thing I learned the hard way was **"desire without knowledge is not good—how much more will hasty feet miss the way!"** Proverbs 19:2 (NIV). I desired to follow Jesus, but I was not knowledgeable yet. When tempted to gamble again on May 7, 2008 (5/7/2008), I gave in and spiraled out of control again. Past sins try to haunt you and get a grip on you when you lose hope.

I remember that night on May 7, 2008 (5/7/2008), when the doctors told us that Andrew had a zero percent chance of living. That news broke me down to the core. I was hurting so bad. It is hard to describe the pain I felt as a loving father. I guess it was similar to the pain God felt when Jesus died on the cross for the sins of mankind. I felt like I needed an outlet to run away from the pain. Furthermore, I was already drifting away from my faith.

That night when they told us my son was going to die, my wife at the time said she was staying at her parents' house, and I went home and cried deeply. A friend later called me and wanted to make me feel better. He thought it was a good idea to invite me to the casino. I needed an escape. So, I went with it, not knowing I was giving the devil a foothold for sin to come back into my life. Over the next four years, that foothold became a stronghold. I became crazy addicted to gambling again, betting up to $1,800 on a single hand in blackjack. I couldn't break the addiction on my own. I needed Jesus to change my heart's desires and free me from this hold.

On July 23, 2012 (7/23/2012), my world came crashing down on me when my wife at the time found out I was gambling behind her back, and that's when she asked for a divorce that night. I was blindsided by it because I never thought this could happen since I told God I would never get a divorce. Since I was forced into it, there was nothing I could do.

The only reason I could get back on my feet was because of the people in my life who pointed me back to the love of God. First and foremost, Jesus Christ, the resurrected King, resurrected my life from death to life again. Second, my parents, Bruce and Sheila, I can't thank them enough for being my unshakeable rocks when I needed them most. I would not be the man I am today without their love and belief in me. They have kept me on this journey of faith and raised me in a way to look to Jesus. **"Start children off on the way they should go, and even when they are old they will not turn from it"** Proverbs 22:6 (NIV). God blessed me immensely when He gave me my parents.

I'd also like to thank my pastors at the time, Craig Beyer, David Quaid a.k.a. DQ, and Steven Furtick. Pastor Craig, pastor and boss at the time, gave me tremendous advice, prayer, and guidance as he walked me through the daily struggle until I was ready to walk on my own. Thank you, sir, for your amazing heart of service in my life! Then my boy for life, DQ, made sure I was never alone. He would invite me to hang out and plan to get my life back on track with healthy physical and spiritual habits. DQ, you are the man, and I mean that! DQ also introduced me to the best pastor on planet Earth, Steven Furtick, from Elevation Church!

Honestly, I do not think Hope in Numbers would exist today without the bold preaching of Pastor Furtick. Thank you so much, sir! Even though we have never met in person, from the bottom of my heart, I want to thank you for following the will of God in your life! I hope to meet you in person and express my gratitude one day. You have delivered some messages that freed me from bondage. If you ever read this book, Pastor Furtick, your birthday is February 19th (2/19). You gave one of the fiercest messages of your career on a verse that matches your birthday from Haggai 2:19 (NLT): **"I am giving you a promise now while the seed is still in the barn. You have not yet harvested your grain, and your grapevines, fig trees, pomegranates, and olive trees have not yet produced their crops. But from this**

day onward I will bless you." This message sticks with me, and I keep it stored in my heart as I continue to count on God to bless my family, this ministry, and all of the people I impact through the message of Hope in Numbers. I thank God for you and your ministry.

Those people have helped change my heart and attitude over the last ten years. With a new perspective on life, my daily routines of hearing messages, and seeing Hope in Numbers, I now have a full grip on hope and control over my life. Whenever I get invited to play poker, which is not very often, I have a new reason to say "yes" and play with an old friend. To be clear, I do not believe gambling is a sin, but it can quickly lead to sinning. Just like drinking alcohol is not a sin, it can lead to it. **"Do not get drunk on wine, which leads to debauchery. Instead, be filled with the Spirit"** Ephesians 5:18 (NIV). You need to know your limits and realize when enough is enough. **"If anyone, then, knows the good they ought to do and doesn't do it, it is sin for them"** James 4:17 (NIV).

I play Texas Hold'em with an old friend sometimes now as a way to be a messenger of light for Jesus. **"For this is what the Lord has commanded us: 'I have made you a light for the Gentiles, that you may bring salvation to the ends of the earth'"** Acts 13:47 (NIV). Now, I see Hope in Numbers in every hand I am dealt, which keeps my spirit focused on the Lord and not on the things of this world. I share Hope in Numbers at the table, invite them to church, and am available to help anybody with addictive habits through the grace of Jesus Christ when they are ready. **"He comforts us in all our troubles so that we can comfort others. When they are troubled, we will be able to give them the same comfort God has given us"** 2 Corinthians 1:4 (NLT).

There is a parallel between the game of Texas Hold'em and life that I want to share with you to help you defeat temptation and set you free from the bondage of any addiction. The wisdom is this; you can still win the hand even if you are dealt bad cards! Let's say you are dealt a 2-7 suite, which is a very bad hand to play poker. The odds are against you to win, but you can still win! Here's how. All you need is a good poker face and the boldness to go ALL IN against your opponent for them to lose hope and fold their cards!

Jesus and my friend, James Jones, helped me come up with this parallel that even when dealt a bad hand in life, you can still win! I was dealt the hand of a dysfunctional heart, diabetes, a disabled son, destructive gambling addiction, and divorce. The only way I've been able to win and not fold is because I go ALL IN for Jesus daily**! "You will seek me and find me when you seek me with ALL your heart"** Jeremiah 29:13 (NIV) (emphasis mine). Go all in with Jesus! Get out of the boat and trust in Him! It is only when you go ALL IN that the enemy will put down his cards and fold to the King of Kings, Jesus Christ!

Disarm the Devil's Schemes

The last lesson I learned from my gambling addiction is how addiction works. I discovered four steps the devil uses to trap us in a stronghold of addiction. We can avoid these four steps if we know what they are and recognize them in our lives. First, the devil tries to get a foothold in your life. Like when you climb a rock wall, there are footholds that you use with your foot to push you up. If you give the devil a foothold in your life, he will use it to step on you and push you down. **"Do not give the devil a foothold"** Ephesians 4:27 (NIV). A foothold is not a very strong grip, but that's where it all starts. That is why the devil wants to take your sinfulness to the next level, which is a mental stronghold.

The battle for sin is won and lost inside the mind. Whatever gets your attention gets you! **"So letting your sinful nature**

control your mind leads to death. But letting the Spirit control your mind leads to life and peace" Romans 8:6 (NLT). Control your thoughts and focus them on Christ and His wonderful grace so that your spirit will be led by God and deceived by your flesh!

The third step of addiction is a heart hold. This is when your desire to sin outweighs those desires for righteousness. **"The human heart is the most deceitful of all things, and desperately wicked. Who really knows how bad it is?"** Jeremiah 17:9 (NLT).

The fourth step, once you have fallen for the other holds, is when the sinful addiction becomes a stronghold in your life. That is when the devil has a full grip on your hope, and you need help from God to rip it back from the enemy's hand. The definition of a stronghold is a vice-like grip.

With His help, Jesus has turned all of my pain for His gain. He has taught me wisdom through my battles. So, now I can help others through their own. We can get a grip back on our Hope and keep it away from the devil's schemes.

Do Not Lose Grip on Your Hope

Well, you've made it to the final teaching section of this book. Congratulations! I hope you enjoy the activities, games, and testimonies in the next section to help you HOLD onto T.R.U.T.H. forever and never lose your grip! I want to quickly review the ways to hold onto this practice with a firm grip. Then I want to explain the five ways the enemy tries to strip your hope away from you.

T ry it
R enew it
U se it
T each it
H old it

Use these five steps to Hold Onto Promises Everywhere! There is a verse in Galatians that the Apostle Paul wrote to a church that was losing grip on hope. He said, **"You were running the race so well. Who has held you back from following the truth?" Galatians 5:7** (NLT).

I want to warn you of some tactics the devil uses to try and keep you from following God's Truth. They are represented by the acronym F.A.L.S.E. and can be illustrated by the five fingers Satan uses to try and rip away your hope.

F ear
A ffliction
L ies
S in
E mptiness

Fear

Do you see the scratches on this book cover? Fear is one of the scratches from his finger that the devil tries to use to get a grip on our hope. As you know, many situations in life naturally arouse fear from within us. The devil knows this to be true. Therefore, he tries to use it to his advantage. Satan tries to steal our hope away by getting us to freeze in fear. The devil will taunt us with fear and make us think fearful thoughts repeatedly. Our best defense against this is to know his tactics. **"In order that Satan might not outwit us. For we are not unaware of his schemes"** 2 Corinthians 2:11 (NIV).

How do we defeat this tactic? Well, the word of God tells us 365 times in the Bible Do not fear. That's exactly the number of days in one year! Let us use God's Word and Hope in Numbers daily to defeat Satan's tactics and destroy fear's grip on our lives. **"For God has not given us a spirit of fear and timidity, but of power, love, and self-discipline"** 2 Timothy 1:7 (NLT). The truth is, being afraid doesn't change God's plan for your life, but living in fear daily could cause you to miss walking out His plan for your life.

When we understand God's unwavering love and forgiveness for us, we have no reason to fear. Our God is a good and Holy Father who protects and watches over His children. **"Such love has no fear, because perfect love expels all fear. If we are afraid, it is for fear of punishment, and this shows that we have not fully experienced his perfect love"** 1 John 4:18 (NLT). God's love for us is immeasurable! Nails didn't hold Jesus to the cross; His love for us did.

Affliction

The second tactic the devil uses to pry away our hope from us is by using affliction. The Word of God tells us, **"Be joyful in hope, patient in affliction, faithful in prayer"** Romans 12:12 (NIV). I've looked up synonyms for affliction, and here is what came up: suffering, difficulty, burden, problem, pain, trouble, and misery. Can you relate to any of these? I bet you can. I relate to all of them. Afflictions distract me from holding onto the wonderful truths of God. The reality is there are afflictions in the world, but numbers are also! Now you can find hope in those numbers to get through any trial! **"We are pressed on every side by troubles, but we are not crushed. We are perplexed, but not driven to despair. We are hunted down but never abandoned by God. We get knocked down, but we are not destroyed"** 2 Corinthians 4:8-9 (NLT).

A dysfunctional heart, diabetes, a disabled son, destructive addiction, and divorce are the 5 D's that the devil has used against me to destroy me. Thank God, I have Hope in Numbers to arm me with God's Word, so I don't lose heart! **"He will cover you with his feathers. He will shelter you with his wings. His**

faithful promises are your armor and protection" Psalm 91:4 (NLT). All of the failures in my life simply became fertilizer for my faith to grow and to become the man I am today. I thank God that He has brought me through every hardship! He is a faithful God!

I am where I am today because I've armed myself with God's Word. I pray you will do the same. So, you can take a stand against the enemy's attacks and win the battle of Hope Wars in your life. Staying strong through your afflictions will make for a glorious testimony one day that will have the power to save many souls. **"For our present troubles are small and won't last very long. Yet they produce for us a glory that vastly outweighs them and will last forever!"** 2 Corinthians 4:17 (NLT).

Lies

The third finger, or tactic, that the devil uses to try to rip our hope away is lies. There is a verse in the Bible that accurately explains the character of Satan. **"He was a murderer from the beginning. He has always hated the truth, because there is no truth in him. When he lies, it is consistent with his character; for he is a liar and the father of lies"** John 8:44 (NLT). The bottom line is that Satan lies, and his lies can cause you to fear, doubt, and tremble at the thought of your future, your current circumstances, and your relationship with God. The devil paints a picture of God as somebody who holds back blessings from you, is looking to punish you for your shortcomings, and as somebody who doesn't care deeply for you. We know this is not the truth about God! We know our God sent His one and only Son to die for us so we can experience heaven with Him for eternity!

It's easy to believe the devil's lies. We can wander into Satan's lies easily, but if we have believed in his lies for quite some time now, it may be increasingly difficult to wander out. His lies are broadcasted around us on secular radio, movies, TV, and more! We must carefully analyze what we listen to and compare it to the Word of God, the source of Truth.

The devil's greatest lie may be that everyone has plenty of time to get right with God. He tries to convince you that sin is fun and that you can live in sin all you want because you can turn to God when you have had plenty of time sinning. That lie can lead you to the destruction of your life. Sin leads to death! Instead, firmly believe in God's Word and experience true life, joy, and peace that surpasses all understanding!

Sin

The fourth finger the devil uses to pry away our hope from us is sin. Sin is an archery term, and it means to miss the mark. If you don't hit the center of the target every time, you sin. In life, we miss the target of God's perfect holiness. Only Jesus was perfect every time. **"For everyone has sinned; we all fall short of God's glorious standard"** Romans 3:23 (NLT). If you've ever said a wrong word, thought of a wrong deed, or committed a wrong action, you have sinned and have fallen short of God's holy and righteous standard.

The evil one will remind you daily of your sinfulness and try to convince you there is no hope. But you know that the devil is a liar! The truth is, **"if we confess our sins, he is faithful and just and will forgive us our sins and purify us from all unrighteousness"** 1 John 1:9 (NIV). Yes, there are still real consequences if you sin, but God is faithful and just and will forgive you if you ask him to. You can truly repent and change your ways through His forgiveness. That is what the grace of God is intended for and allows you to do. Grace means unmerited favor, and the grace to be forgiven for past, present, and future sins give the opportunity to change your ways for the better. As a sinner saved by grace, we must stop remembering what God has forgotten. **"As far as the east is from the west, so far has he removed our transgressions from us"** Psalms 103:12 (NIV).

Here's the thing. If the devil can convince you that when you sin, you fall out of favor with God, then he likely has a firm grip on your hope and can pry it away from you. Refuse to let him get a grip on your hope because of sin! The devil will try to condemn you to hell every time you sin, now or from the past. When we read the Word of God, we know it says, **"Therefore, there is now no condemnation for those who are in Christ Jesus"** Romans 8:1 (NIV). Let's not let our past, present, or future sins separate us from the love of God.

As Christians, we will never be sinless, but we will sin less and less as we follow Christ. Remember this truth—Jesus will never love you more or less than He does right now. So get back on your saddle when you fail, and make the adjustments to do better next time. **"For though the righteous fall seven times, they rise again, but the wicked stumble when calamity strikes"** Proverbs 24:16 (NIV).

Emptiness

The fifth finger, or thumb, the devil uses to pry away our hope is emptiness. The devil is a liar and tries to convince you that those sinful desires will fill your voids in life. But we all know that worldly pursuits will leave you feeling empty inside. There is a God-shaped hole in our hearts that only is fully satisfied when God fills it with His loving presence. Other things in this world are temporary fixes and are not everlasting. **"Do not love this world nor the things it offers you, for when you love the world, you do not have the love of the Father in you"** 1 John 2:15 (NLT).

The world tries to fill our God-shaped void with things like money, success, sex, drugs, power, and more. The devil tries to get us to pursue these things, and they leave us feeling empty or depressed because it's never enough. **"For the world offers only a craving for physical pleasure, a craving for everything we see, and pride in our achievements and possessions. These are not from the Father, but are from this world. And this world is fading away, along with everything that people crave. But anyone who does what pleases God will live forever"** 1 John 2:16-17 (NLT).

In this world, you will find people who look successful on the outside but have empty souls inside. The reason is they put all the things of this world inside their void, only to discover that we were designed to have God at the center of our lives. Pursue God with all of your heart and feel true satisfaction by serving, worshiping, and being in a close, loving relationship with the Creator of this universe and your soul.

Hopeful

When you make it a habit to hold onto and hoard God's promises in your heart, you will complete the process of Hope in Numbers, and you will be HOPE-ful! You will be filled with hope in all your circumstances! **"May the God of hope fill you with all joy and peace as you trust in him, so that you may overflow with hope by the power of the Holy Spirit"** Romans 15:13 (NIV).

No longer will F.A.L.S.E. beliefs get the best grip on your life. You will be able to overpower the enemy's grip and secure your hope in the Lord, keeping His promises close to your heart all the days of your life! Hope in Numbers can help you do this and do it well!

"Do you not know? Have you not heard? The Lord is the everlasting God, the Creator of the ends of the earth. He

will not grow tired or weary, and his understanding no one can fathom. He gives strength to the weary and increases the power of the weak. Even youths grow tired and weary, and young men stumble and fall; but those who hope in the Lord will renew their strength. They will soar on wings like eagles; they will run and not grow weary, they will walk and not be faint." Isaiah 40:28-31 (NIV)

Holding Onto Promises Everywhere Challenge

Do you remember in 2015 when there was a viral craze across social media called the ALS Ice Bucket Challenge? It was a challenge that spread like wildfire when somebody made a video to challenge a friend or family member to donate money to the ALS Foundation or get a bucket of ice water poured on them. The friend or family member had forty-eight hours to complete the challenge on video. The purpose was to raise awareness of ALS and to get people to donate to the nonprofit organization. People loved it, and it went on for months.

I thought for our last challenge of this book, we could pull off something similar that could spread awareness of Holding Onto Promises Everywhere in numbers. I'm challenging us Christians to take on the Holding Onto Promises Everywhere Challenge! It is very similar to the ALS Ice Bucket Challenge, but we find a number, quote a verse on video, and then challenge somebody else to do the same. They would have forty-eight hours to find a number out in the world and quote the scripture that goes with it, or else the HOPE died with them! What do you say? Will you accept the challenge? Let's change this world for Jesus, one number and one person at a time! Let's go!

Read a testimony I received from a teenager from our local church and how making a Hope in Numbers video helped her to memorize a verse that stays with her to this day. Her name is Haley. Read what she had to say:

Hope in Numbers

I have to admit when I was first introduced to Hope in Numbers and Gordon's group, I was in shock! It was pretty cool how quickly Bible verses popped into their heads and poured out of their mouths. I listened in amazement thinking, "I wish I could be able to do that!" Little did I know that with a little effort and some repetition, I would soon see through the same vision as them.

My first Hope in Numbers video was at the mall. We were just walking around strolling through the stores, and I was hearing others quote verses from memory. I followed along, quietly admiring what they were doing. We then walked into a clothing store and wandered around looking for numbers. We finally came up to a shirt hanging on a rack with a large 58 on it. Gordon immediately pointed at me and said, "This one is yours!" He pulled out his phone to record my first Hope in Numbers video.

I promise you I could feel my hands trembling. I never thought I could do it! At first, I tried and tried but couldn't get it right. But after a few more takes, it clicked! The verse finally came out right! I quoted Romans 5:8, and a rush of excitement flowed through me when I did it. At that moment, that verse became etched in me forever.

I've learned that Hope in Numbers is a process; it doesn't just miraculously come over you right away, but it does come! For me, it came after 12 or 13 tries. Just trust the process. Because for me it doesn't matter how long it takes. It matters the effort I make to get there. To this day, Romans 5:8, ***"But God demonstrates His own love for us in this: While we were still sinners, Christ*** *died for us"* *pops up in my head all the time when I see the number 58. Street signs, jersey numbers, times of the day, everywhere! It's a process. Practice it until you get it. Trust me, it's the best thing when you can see a verse out in your daily life. It's seeing Jesus in our world, and it's a blessing that is changing my life.*

Final Words

It's been an honor to serve you in writing this book. I hope it inspires you to take your faith journey to an entirely new level! **"Let your roots grow down into him, and let your lives be built on him. Then your faith will grow strong in the truth you were taught, and you will overflow with thankfulness"** Colossians 2:7 (NLT). Remember to be hopeful always because our God is good. He loves you and wants the very best for your life.

I encourage you to use this book to keep your faith with you, no matter your circumstances. No matter what the world throws or takes away from you, you will always have God's Word and encouragement in your heart to bless you. Just like the Book of Revelation was figuratively written to Jewish believers so Roman rulers wouldn't understand it fully and take it away, I believe Hope in Numbers will be a way for us Christians to always have God's Word with us no matter what! The world can try to take our Bibles away from us, but they will never be able to take away our stored treasure in the many scriptures we have memorized and the memories of God's Word through numbers!

It's been a blessed duty of mine to write this book. I toiled but completed it with joy in my heart, knowing that it will soon bless you, the reader of this book! I pray that your journey is filled with many Hope in Numbers stories, joyous moments with the Lord, and the firm belief that the Lord is with you always.

He never leaves you or forsakes you. May God bless you in your journey of seeing hope in every number! There is nothing in this world that can separate you from the Word of God. You will never see numbers the same way again!

Testimonies, Activities, Games and Verses

The purpose of this section is to give you some practical tools with which to use your new five-step process of Holding Onto Promises Everywhere! Enjoy these fun ideas and use them with your friends and family. You will be glad you did. Also, in this section you will read a few more testimonies from people who use Hope in Numbers in their life! Hear how it has blessed them. Lastly, use this section to find Bible verses for numbers you see out in the world. You will find scripture for jersey number Bible verses, as well as Birthday Bible verses for every day of the year!

This is just a glimpse of some of the activities, games, and even Bible verses for different days of the year. If you would like more activities, games, and Birthday Bible verses for specific days then please visit: www.hopeinnumbers.net/more

Testimonies

Numbers are everywhere in our world. The question is do we see them and what do we do with them? Over the past couple years, Gordon has helped open my eyes to see Jesus through numbers every day. For me, whenever I step foot onto the baseball field, I immediately feel God's love when I see Hope in Numbers! I look out at the signs on the outfield fence and I see 330 ft on the right field fence. Right away, I find wisdom in Jesus. John 3:30: **"He must increase and I must decrease."**

When I see hope in those numbers, I get on fire and am ready to play the game of baseball for Jesus! I play

for an audience of one, and with that perspective I can even help change my teammate's hearts through God's love. God's hope is everywhere, and all we have to do is look! I know that God is with me in my games and on the field and throughout my whole life! Seeing those numbers helps me see Him every day and keeps me on fire for God!

Noah Burgarello

As a college student, I have been able to see Hope In Numbers everywhere I go on campus. I am studying Business Finance at Grand Canyon University, and finding Hope in Numbers brings me encouragement all day, every day.

My first class starts at 8:25 a.m. so as I walk to class I remember Romans 8:25. Later, I have class in the engineering building in room 330, and I remember John 3:30 before I walk into that classroom every day. Whether I have a lecture or a test, finding Hope in Numbers brings me a quick source of encouragement to keep my focus on God.

Even when school and life get busy and stressful, God finds a way to speak to me through the numbers I see. As a finance major, I see countless numbers every day. Whether I'm doing homework, taking a test, or listening in class, God constantly shows me His love through the verses I find in the numbers. God has been using these verses to constantly refresh me and to pick me up on the hardest of days. Using numbers to see God's promises keeps me going and always reminds me of His constant presence in my life. Even on the hardest days with the hardest problems, God brings me hope through numbers.

Marco Burgarello

When I first was introduced to Gordon, little did I know the way I viewed the scriptures was forever going to change. I have the privilege to work in the same company as Gordon, and we connected when we found out that we both love the Lord. He proceeded by stating scripture while looking at the time on the clock right above us. I thought the way he can connect any number to scripture was absolutely amazing. He asked for my birthdate and quickly stated my Birthday verse, **"And let the peace of Christ rule in your hearts, to which indeed you were called in one body and be thankful"** (Colossians 3:15).

After watching Gordon quote scripture after scripture with every number around him, I knew I wanted to do the same. I started off just memorizing my birthday scripture, and then little by little, I started seeing scripture all around me. At times it was really difficult for me, but I just felt like I needed to try harder. I later came across James 1:5 which states, **"If any of you lack wisdom, let him ask God, who gives generously to all without reproach, and it will be given to him."** I learned the more you love God's Word, the easier it will be to state scripture with every number you see.

What amazed me the most is the love Gordon has for the Word of God. It's really hard to find people nowadays that just love to dive into the Word of God, yet alone *memorize the scriptures. From that moment on, Gordon and I have created this great friendship; I like to consider him to be my brother.*

I have the honor of being a youth leader at my home church, and at times I am given a schedule for when I will be preaching the Word. After diving into the Word of God and prayer, I can't tell you how many times I have gone to Gordon to ask for help or even additional scripture for my sermon. I love the analogies that he gives me to add onto what I'm speaking. The best part is when I share my sermons I like to add how Hope in Numbers works with our youth and they absolutely love it.

I'd like to share that I love the way Gordon believes in me and how proud he gets when I preach or even speak about the word of God. Hope in Numbers has made a change in my life. This past May, I was blessed to marry the woman of my dreams and I had Gordon right there next to me as one of my groomsmen. When the days were coming closer, he would have a verse for however many days I had left to tie the knot. One of the best verses he stated was on my wedding day (May 26th) which really connected to what God was doing and how I prayed my marriage would be. Gordon stated Ephesians 5:25-26: **"Husbands love your wives, as Christ loved the church and gave himself up for her. That he might sanctify her, having cleansed her by the washing of water with the word."**

That scripture that Gordon stated was so powerful I had to use it for my vows. So reader, I encourage you first to love the Word of God, seek Him and you'll see that when you start connecting numbers all around you wherever you go, you will see that Hope in Numbers can change your life also.

Jesus Alvarado

When I first started following Gordon on Instagram a couple of years ago, I knew right away that I was going to love his posts because he had such a passion for the Word! Not only was I impressed, but I knew right away he had a God-given talent to share the Word through Hope in Numbers. He was on fire for Jesus! I have never met Gordon in person, but his love for God, the Word and his family was somethings I was drawn to! Hope in Numbers has taught me that God's Word is everywhere we look and wherever there are numbers there is Hope!

Being a Christian all of my life and accepting Christ into my heart when I was eight years old, and hearing the Word from childhood till now, I always knew the scriptures and heard them repeated in the pulpit many times and even memorized them. The only difference was I didn't really know the chapter and verse, but now when I see the numbers, I know there is a scripture behind it. For example, when I see the numbers 1, 2, 3, I now see James 1:2-3! When I travel and stay in hotel rooms, it never fails that I get a room such as 413, for Philippians 4:13, or 323, for Romans 3:23, or 322, for Lamentations 3:22 and on and on it goes!

When I see these numbers, His Word becomes real! One more thing that Hope in Numbers has taught me is that every month and day there is a scripture to stand on! I am thankful that every month and day there will be a powerful scripture for that day! Literally from 1-1 to 12-31!

I have memorized so many scriptures in the last two years, something I never really thought about! It's life-changing! I am so very thankful to Gordon and Hope in Numbers for opening up my eyes to see His Word in any number!

Love in Christ, Doe Doe

Hope in Numbers has been great way for me to learn scriptures in the Bible. I grew up in the church and from a young age, I would read my Bible on a regular basis. Even though I read the Bible frequently, I was never able to remember where certain scriptures were in the Bible. I would have awesome talks with friends about Jesus, and certain verses would pop into my mind. I would say a paraphrased version of the scripture because I could not remember the verse word for word or where it was in the Bible. I would tell my friends, "You know, that verse in the New Testament."

When Gordon introduced me to Hope in Numbers, it all seemed to click. I found that it was easy for me to memorize where scriptures were by relating the numbers to the time. For example, I teach 6th grade and I have four different classes that switch hourly. I learned a verse for every hour that my classes switch. So now, even if I am having a rough day at school and students are not doing what they are supposed to be doing, instead of getting mad or upset, scripture pops into my head and reconnects me back to God.

The school day ends at 3:30 p.m. every day and the verse I have connected to that time is John 3:30 (NIV), which states: **"He must become greater; I must become less."** *This is always a great way to end my day because it reminds me of my purpose. I am teaching not for my glory, but for His glory. It does not matter what kind of day I have. I am here for a reason and that is to make Jesus famous at my school and with my students. Thank you so much, Gordon, for Hope in Numbers.*

Zachary Hamrick

I've known Gordon for three years and over the past three years I have gotten to know a few things about him. God has blessed him with an unbelievable brain that he uses to further the Kingdom. Gordon is a great example of what a father, husband, and servant of Christ looks like. I see this in his children, as well as the students that he leads in the high school ministry.

Hope in Numbers isn't something that Gordon created, but rather something that God has given Gordon the responsibility of using his brain to create. Gordon's gift is accessible to anyone that puts their mind to it and he constantly encourages people to give it a try. As a sports fan, I constantly remember scores and stats of players and Gordon has influenced me to see God's Word through those stats and numbers. I am a fan of Hope in Numbers, but an even bigger fan of Gordon Wickert and the follower of Christ he exemplifies.

Matt Newman Numbers determine so much of our lives; the time when we have to leave for school or work, the date of our next appointment, our age and weight. It wasn't until I first spoke to Gordon about Hope in Numbers that I started to see those same numbers as a way to connect with God's Word constantly. I no longer just see numbers as a way to dictate the places I need to be or when I have to pick up my kids for school, I see them as a way to **"meditate on His law day and night"** *(Psalm 1:2 NIV). I believe that this method of seeing Hope in Numbers can help anyone who wants to remain in His word at all times.*

Pastor Leo Galarza

My birthday is January 16th and now that I am in my thirties, it doesn't matter that much to me; it's just another day on the calendar. Or is it? That's where a dear brother in Christ offered me so much encouragement. My brother in Christ, Gordon Wickert, through his faithful obedience to the Holy Spirit has enlightened the eyes of my understanding! He explained to me that my birthday reads 1/16 which can remind me of a famous verse in Romans 1:16 (NLT): **"For I am not ashamed of this Good News about Christ. It is the power of God at work, saving everyone who believes—the Jew first and also the Gentile."**

A simple arrangement of numbers that are truly personal to me, but have become much more a reminder of a truth found in the Bible! Why just stop at my birthday? I was on a mission to look for Bible verses everywhere, from birthdays, major holidays, anniversaries, and more! Gordon found Hope in my license plate number one day when he was behind me in traffic. He would also send me pictures and videos of numbers found in grocery stores, receipts, street addresses, sports scores and more!

Hope in Numbers is a life-changer! In addition to increasing my faith, it has prompted an earnest spirit to share this method of memorizing scripture with others. I tried using the steps Gordon laid out and it became almost like clockwork. When the clock strikes just past noon (12:02 to be exact), I think of Romans 12:2 (NLT): ***"Don't copy the behavior and customs of this world, but let God transform you into a new person by changing the way you think. Then you will learn to know God's will for you, which is good and pleasing and perfect."***

Thanks to Hope in Numbers, I have modeled this method of memorizing and retaining scripture and even teaching it to my family and friends. I have three sons, and they enjoy looking for numbers everywhere we go! Hope in Numbers truly is a method God is using, through the faithful leadership of Gordon, to help me change the way I think! Learning how to memorize scripture through Hope in Numbers let's God will lead in my life ***"which is good and pleasing and perfect!"***

Holding Onto Promises Everywhere,

Eddie Hyatt

Chapter 6 - Hold It

Activities
Return To Bethel Activity

This activity goes along with the Bible story from Genesis 28 where Jacob was running from Esau because he had stolen the blessing. Jacob renamed this place that was once called Luz to Bethel. **"He named that place Bethel (which means "house of God"), although it was previously called Luz"** Genesis 28:19 (NLT). So Jacob renamed the place because he knew God was with him through it all and I believe God wants to rename some places and events in your life too. So here's how you can return to Bethel in your own life. I want you to think about some important dates in your life, good or bad, and see what promises and truths are hidden in the numbers of those dates. Rename those bad dates with hope and the good days with even more joy!

Good day examples: Birthdays, wedding or dating anniversaries, the day you accepted Jesus or the day you were baptized. Bad day examples: Date of the death of a loved one, divorced date, lost a job date. Use the space down below to give this activity a try and return to Bethel in your own life!

Event _____ + Date _____ =
Bible Verse _____
_____
_____

Event _____ + Date _____ =
Bible Verse _____
_____
_____

Event _____ + Date _____ =
Bible Verse _____
_____
_____

Event _____ + Date _____ =
Bible Verse _____
_____
_____

Event _____ + Date _____ =
Bible Verse _____
_____
_____

Birthday Verse Activity

In this activity, I want you to get a blank calendar to fill in. Once you have the calendar, set out on a mission to fill in every date with the birthdays of people you know. Then share with them their Birthday Bible Verse when the day comes. You can use this book to give them their Birthday Bible verse or simply memorize it before you tell them! Make it your challenge to find somebody to encourage with God's Word for every day of the year, all 365 days! This will be a really fun and exciting way to share Hope in Numbers with your friends and family!

Strategic Verse Placement Activity

This activity will turn your world into a weapon against the evil one. Start by getting a few sticky tabs that you can write on. You are going to want to write the name of a specific book in the Bible, such as "Romans" on the note and place that sticky note next to a digital clock somewhere in your home, car or

Chapter 6 - Hold It

work station. Now, every minute your clock turns you can be reminded of Bible verses that come from that book! For example, I have "Proverbs" on a sticky tab above my car radio clock, "Romans" on my microwave clock, "James" on my stove clock, and "Matthew" over my clock at work. Every clock I have gives me a timely word from God throughout my day. You can do this too! Time will no longer be against you, but for you!

The second thing you can do with strategic verse placement is write the chapter and verse number you want to memorize. Then place it on or by what the verse is talking about. A few examples would be:

1. On any door in your house write "Revelation 3:20" then memorize the verse that says, **"Look! I stand at the door and knock. If you hear my voice and open the door, I will come in, and we will share a meal together as friends."** Placing this verse on a door will help you memorize what the verse is about.

2. On the mirror in your bathroom, place a sticky tab and write "James 1:22-24" on it which says, **"But don't just listen to God's word. You must do what it says. Otherwise, you are only fooling yourselves. For if you listen to the word and don't obey, it is like glancing at your face in a mirror. You see yourself, walk away, and forget what you look like."** This should help you memorize these verses when you glance in the mirror every day.

3. Next to the sink in the bathroom for when you wash your hands you can write on a sticky note "Proverbs 11:25" which says, **"The generous will prosper; those who refresh others will themselves be refreshed."**

4. In your car's rear view mirror on a small tab write "Philippians 3:13" which says, **"Brothers, I do not**

179

Hope in Numbers

consider that I have made it my own. But one thing I do: forgetting what lies behind and straining forward to what lies ahead."

Do you see how this activity can turn clocks and other objects into reminders of God's scripture? This is a powerful activity that is sure to bring you continuous blessings as you memorize, and put into practice more scripture!

Games

Use the Bible verses in the back to help you with these games. These games are really fun in youth groups or families that want to be see and practice Hope in Numbers. Try them out yourself!

Bible Streak

I've learned from having a teenager daughter and being around the younger generation a lot that they care more about what they call "streaks" on Snapchat, working out, or days they've dated somebody, than about getting into a good streak of seeing and reading God's Word. Streaks are consecutive days that you do something without missing a day. So in this game, take your streak number for whatever it is you are streaking and transform the streak number into a Bible verse. Now you can share the streak number Bible verse with the person you are on the streak with. First person to share the Bible streak verse in the morning will win the Bible Streak game for that day!

Example, let's say you have a streak with your best friend at sixty-five today. Look in this book under Jersey verses and see what there is for the number sixty-five. It would be Deuteronomy 6:5 (NIV): **"Love the Lord your God with all your heart and with all your soul and with all your strength."** Boom! Start a Bible streak for Jesus today and win against your friends daily to share the first verse. #BibleStreaksforJesus

Chapter 6 - Hold It

Road Trips with Hope in Numbers

How many of you remember playing the game "50 States" while on a long road trip to pass time? The object of the game was to find as many different states on license plates that you could and whoever found the most, won. Well let's take that game next level and instead of looking for states, let's look for Bible verses in those license plates!

Take this Hope in Numbers book with you on your road trips and use the verses in the back or the YouVersion Bible app to help you find verses you know! There's a few ways to play this game. First, play it like the "50 States" game by splitting the car up into two teams. One team can look for odd numbers and the other can look for even numbers. Just like a bingo card, mark off the ones you find in this book in the Jersey verse section, or on a piece of paper/notes app on your phone. The team with the most verses found in one hour wins! And only allow license plates and billboards for this game because using the exit sign numbers are too easy to find!

The second way to play this game on a road trip, or just on a drive somewhere, would be like the game "Eye Spy with My Little Eye". Take turns picking a Bible verse number to look for, but first read the verse out loud for the car to hear. Then someone can say, "I spy with my little eye for the numbers 831." Romans 8:31 (NIV) says, "**If God is for us, who can be against us?**" Take turns with everyone playing in the car. Spend a couple minutes per round looking for that number out in the world. If you find it, you get the point and the most points win!

Hope War

Most people I bet know how to play the classic game "War" with a full deck of playing cards. Hope War is very similar, but with a twist. The game is played with two players. You split up the entire

Hope in Numbers

deck of fifty-two cards so that you both have twenty-six cards. Each of you places a card faceup and the first person to quote a Bible verse with the two numbers wins those two cards! This is an open book game so use the verses in the back or the YouVersion Bible app if you don't already have the verses memorized. People with the most verses memorized will have the advantage! The player with the most cards at the end wins the Hope War!

Hope in Numbers Fire Trick

People love card magic tricks, but what if instead of showing magic, you showed them wisdom! Ask someone to pick two cards then quote a Bible verse matching the card numbers. This trick will actually help them in life and not just entertain them. I go around with a deck of cards and dice and ask people if they want to see the Hope in Numbers Fire Trick and they get blessed with a timely Bible verse! To be able to do this, you need to spend some time memorizing all the possible outcomes of this trick.

I challenge you to memorize all the jersey number Bible verses in the back and then you could do most two card tricks in the deck and all dice rolls. Memorize just two verses per week for one year. You would have 104 verses memorized!

Church Campus Bingo

Turn you church's campus in to a huge bingo board of Hope in Numbers! This is a blast for church youth groups or kid's ministries. You can use numbers that are already posted all over your campus or you can place numbers on index cards all over the campus. Create teams, however you want. Make a bingo board on Word or Excel and send them out. You can make them take pictures or videos of them quoting the Bible verse for a bonus point. The first group to win their board is the Church Bingo Champions!

Chapter 6 - Hold It

A Minute to Spit It

My youth group loves this game and they have even helped me name it. In this game, you pick any random Bible verse. I've downloaded the free Chegg Flashcards app on my phone and made flashcards with all the verses 1-99. Or you could do this on regular index cards too. On one side of the flash card put only the number for the verse, and on the other side write out the whole Bible verse and reference.

You pick a person to come to the front of the group, and show the person only the side with the numbers on it, and then say "GO!" He or she has one minute to preach on that Bible verse on the flash card. If they don't know it, you can show them the back of the index card to preach on it. It's really cool and fun to see what kind of wisdom people come up with on the spot.

BIRTHDAY BIBLE VERSES / VERSE OF THE DAY

January

1/1
"Oh, the joys of those who do not follow the advice of the wicked, or stand around with sinners, or join in with mockers. But they delight in the law of the LORD, meditating on it day and night. They are like trees planted along the riverbank, bearing fruit each season. Their leaves never wither, and they prosper in all they do."
(**Psalms 1:1-3** NLT)

1/2
Consider it pure joy, my brothers and sisters, whenever you face trials of many kinds,
(**James 1:2** NIV)

1/3
"That person is like a tree planted by streams of water, which yields its fruit in season and whose leaf does not wither— whatever they do prospers."
(**Psalm 1:3** NIV)

1/4
He comforts us in all our troubles so that we can comfort others. When they are troubled, we will be able to give them the same comfort God has given us.
(**2 Corinthians 1:4** NLT)

1/5
If any of you lacks wisdom, you should ask God, who gives generously to all without finding fault, and it will be given to you.
(**James 1:5** NIV)

1/6
being confident of this, that he who began a good work in you will carry it on to completion until the day of Christ Jesus.
(**Philippians 1:6** NIV)

1/7
For God has not given us a spirit of fear and timidity, but of power, love, and self-discipline.
(2 **Timothy 1:7** NLT)

1/8
Keep this Book of the Law always on your lips; meditate on it day and night, so that you may be careful to do everything written in it. Then you will be prosperous and successful.
(**Joshua 1:8** NIV)

1/9
Have I not commanded you? Be strong and courageous. Do not be afraid; do not be discouraged, for the Lord your God will be with you wherever you go."
(**Joshua 1:9** NIV)

1/10
Am I now trying to win the approval of human beings, or of God? Or am I trying to please people? If I were still trying to please people, I would not be a servant of Christ.
(**Galatians 1:10** NIV)

1/11
And may the LORD, the God of your ancestors, multiply you a thousand times more and bless you as he promised!
(**Deuteronomy 1:11** NLT)

1/12
Blessed is the one who perseveres under trial because, having stood the test, that person will receive the crown of life that the Lord has promised to those who love him.
(**James 1:12** NIV)

1/13
"So prepare your minds for action and exercise self-control. Put all your hope in the gracious salvation that will come to you when Jesus Christ is revealed to the world."
(1 **Peter 1:13** NLT)

1/14
"The Word became flesh and made his dwelling among us. We have seen his glory, the glory of the one and only Son, who came from the Father, full of grace and truth."
(**John 1:14** NIV)

1/15
Christ is the visible image of the invisible God. He existed before anything was created and is supreme over all creation,
(**Colossians 1:15** NLT)

1/16
For I am not ashamed of this Good News about Christ. It is the power of God at work, saving everyone who believes—the Jew first and also the Gentile.
(**Romans 1:16** NLT)

1/17
Every good and perfect gift is from above, coming down from the Father of the heavenly lights, who does not change like shifting shadows.
(**James 1:17** NIV)

1/18
For the message of the cross is foolishness to those who are perishing, but to us who are being saved it is the power of God.
(1 **Corinthians 1:18** NIV)

1/19
Cling to your faith in Christ, and keep your conscience clear. For some people have deliberately violated their consciences; as a result, their faith has been shipwrecked.
(1 **Timothy 1:19** NLT)

1/20
"For I fully expect and hope that I will never be ashamed, but that I will continue to be bold for Christ, as I have been in the past. And I trust that my life will bring honor to Christ, whether I live or die."
(**Philippians 1:20** NLT)

1/21
For to me, to live is Christ and to die is gain.
(**Philippians 1:21** NIV)

1/22
"Yet now he has reconciled you to himself through the death of Christ in his physical body. As a result, he has brought you into his own presence, and you are holy and blameless as you stand before him without a single fault."
(**Colossians 1:22** NLT)

1/23
"But you must continue to believe this truth and stand firmly in it. Don't drift away from the assurance you received when you heard the Good News. The Good News has been preached all over the world, and I, Paul, have been appointed as God's servant to proclaim it."
(**Colossians 1:23** NLT)

1/24
But that does not mean we want to dominate you by telling you how to put your faith into practice. We want to work together with you so you will be full of joy, for it is by your own faith that you stand firm.
(2 **Corinthians 1:24** NLT)

1/25
But whoever looks intently into the perfect law that gives freedom, and continues in it—not forgetting what they have heard, but doing it—they will be blessed in what they do.
(**James 1:25** NIV)

1/26
Then God said, "Let us make mankind in our image, in our likeness, so that they may rule over the fish in the sea and the birds in the sky, over the livestock and all the wild animals, and over all the creatures that move along the ground."
(**Genesis 1:26** NIV)

1/27
Whatever happens, conduct yourselves in a manner worthy of the gospel of Christ. Then, whether I come and see you or only hear about you in my absence, I will know that you stand firm in the one Spirit, striving together as one for the faith of the gospel
(**Philippians 1:27** NIV)

1/28
So we tell others about Christ, warning everyone and teaching everyone with all the wisdom God has given us. We want to present them to God, perfect in their relationship to Christ.
(**Colossians 1:28** NLT)

1/29
That's why I work and struggle so hard, depending on Christ's mighty power that works within me.
(**Colossians 1:29** NLT)

1/30
God has united you with Christ Jesus. For our benefit God made him to be wisdom itself. Christ made us right with God; he made us pure and holy, and he freed us from sin.
(1 **Corinthians 1:30** NLT)

1/31
Therefore, as it is written: "Let the one who boasts boast in the Lord."
(1 **Corinthians 1:31** NIV)

February

2/1
"So we must listen very carefully to the truth we have heard, or we may drift away from it."
(**Hebrews 2:1** NLT)

2/2
Then make me truly happy by agreeing wholeheartedly with each other, loving one another, and working together with one mind and purpose.
(**Philippians 2:2** NLT)

2/3
Don't be selfish; don't try to impress others. Be humble, thinking of others as better than yourselves.
(**Philippians 2:3** NLT)

2/4
Don't look out only for your own interests, but take an interest in others, too.
(**Philippians 2:4** NLT)

2/5
You must have the same attitude that Christ Jesus had.
(**Philippians 2:5** NLT)

2/6
Those who say they live in God should live their lives as Jesus did.
(1 **John 2:6** NLT)

2/7
rooted and built up in him, strengthened in the faith as you were taught, and overflowing with thankfulness.
(**Colossians 2:7** NIV)

2/8
For it is by grace you have been saved, through faith—and this is not from yourselves, it is the gift of God
(**Ephesians 2:8** NIV)

2/9
However, as it is written: "What no eye has seen, what no ear has heard, and what no human mind has conceived" — the things God has prepared for those who love him—
(1 **Corinthians 2:9** NIV)

2/10
For we are God's masterpiece. He has created us anew in Christ Jesus, so we can do the good things he planned on for us long ago.
(**Ephesians 2:10** NLT)

2/11
For the grace of God has appeared that offers salvation to all people.
(**Titus 2:11** NIV)

2/12
Speak and act as those who are going to be judged by the law that gives freedom,
(**James 2:12** NIV)

2/13
"For God is working in you, giving you the desire and the power to do what pleases him."
(**Philippians 2:13** NLT)

2/14
He canceled the record of the charges against us and took it away by nailing it to the cross.
(**Colossians 2:14** NLT)

2/15
He who was seated on the throne said, "I am making everything new!" Then he said, "Write this down, for these words are trustworthy and true."
(**Revelation 21:5** NIV)

2/16
And he also said, "It is finished! I am the Alpha and the Omega—the Beginning and the End. To all who are thirsty I will give freely from the springs of the water of life. (**Revelation 21:6** NLT)

2/17
When Jesus heard this, he told them, "Healthy people don't need a doctor—sick people do. I have come to call not those who think they are righteous, but those who know they are sinners." (**Mark 2:17** NLT)

2/18
But someone will say, "You have faith; I have deeds." Show me your faith without deeds, and I will show you my faith by my deeds.
(**James 2:18** NIV)

2/19
So now you Gentiles are no longer strangers and foreigners. You are citizens along with all of God's holy people. You are members
of God's family.
(**Ephesians 2:19** NLT)

2/20
I have been crucified with Christ and I no longer live, but Christ lives in me. The life I now live in the body, I live by faith in the Son of God, who loved me and gave himself for me.
(**Galatians 2:20** NIV)

2/21
"I do not treat the grace of God as meaningless. For if keeping the law could make us right with God, then there was no need for Christ to die."
(**Galatians 2:21** NLT)

2/22
He sang: "The LORD is my rock, my fortress, and my savior;
(2 **Samuel 22:2** NLT)

2/23
my God is my rock, in whom I find protection. He is my shield, the power that saves me, and my place of safety. He is my refuge, my savior, the one who saves me from violence.
(2 **Samuel 22:3** NLT)

2/24
He personally carried our sins in his body on the cross so that we can be dead to sin and live for what is right. By his wounds you are healed.
(1 **Peter 2:24** NLT)

Hope in Numbers

2/25
"Once you were like sheep who wandered away. But now you have turned to your Shepherd, the Guardian of your souls."
(1 **Peter 2:25** NLT)

2/26
"As the body without the spirit is dead, so faith without deeds is dead."
(**James 2:26** NIV)

2/27
But you have received the Holy Spirit, and he lives within you, so you don't need anyone to teach you what is true. For the Spirit teaches you everything you need to know, and what he teaches is true—it is not a lie. So just as he has taught you, remain in fellowship with Christ.
(1 **John 2:27** NLT)

2/28
You have shown me the way of life, and you will fill me with the joy of your presence.'
(**Acts 2:28** NLT)

2/29
Blessed are those who are generous, because they feed the poor.
(**Proverbs 22:9** NLT)

March

3/1
Therefore, holy brothers and sisters, who share in the heavenly calling, fix your thoughts on Jesus, whom we acknowledge as our apostle and high priest.
(**Hebrews 3:1** NIV)

3/2
Set your minds on things above, not on earthly things.
(**Colossians 3:2** NIV)

3/3
But you, Lord, are a shield around me, my glory, the One who lifts my head high.
(**Psalm 3:3** NIV)

3/4
a time to weep and a time to laugh, a time to mourn and a time to dance,
(**Ecclesiastes 3:4** NIV)

3/5
Trust in the Lord with all your heart and lean not on your own understanding;
(**Proverbs 3:5** NIV)

3/6
Seek his will in all you do, and he will show you which path to take.
(**Proverbs 3:6** NLT)

3/7
I once thought these things were valuable, but now I consider them worthless because of what Christ has done.
(**Philippians 3:7** NLT)

3/8
Prove by the way you live that you have repented of your sins and turned to God.
(**Matthew 3:8** NLT)

3/9
The Lord is not slow in keeping his promise, as some understand slowness. Instead he is patient with you, not wanting anyone to perish, but everyone to come to repentance.
(**2 Peter 3:9** NIV)

3/10
I want to know Christ—yes, to know the power of his resurrection and participation in his sufferings, becoming like him in his death,
(**Philippians 3:10** NIV)

3/11
He has made everything beautiful in its time. He has also set eternity in the human heart; yet no one can fathom what God has done from beginning to end.
(**Ecclesiastes 3:11** NIV)

3/12
Therefore, since we have such a hope, we are very bold.
(2 **Corinthians 3:12** NIV)

3/13
No, dear brothers and sisters, I have not achieved it, but I focus on this one thing: Forgetting the past and looking forward to what lies ahead,
(**Philippians 3:13** NLT)

3/14
I press on toward the goal to win the prize for which God has called me heavenward in Christ Jesus.
(Philippians 3:14 NIV)

3/15
Let the peace of Christ rule in your hearts, since as members of one body you were called to peace. And be thankful.
(Colossians 3:15 NIV)

3/16
For God so loved the world that he gave his one and only Son, that whoever believes in him shall not perish but have eternal life.
(John 3:16 NIV)

3/17
For the Lord is the Spirit, and wherever the Spirit of the Lord is, there is freedom.
(2 Corinthians 3:17 NLT)

3/18
Do not be afraid or discouraged, for the Lord will personally go ahead of you. He will be with you; he will neither fail you nor abandon you."
(Deuteronomy 31:8 NLT)

3/19
Repent, then, and turn to God, so that your sins may be wiped out, that times of refreshing may come from the Lord,
(Acts 3:19 NIV)

3/20
Now to him who is able to do immeasurably more than all we ask or imagine, according to his power that is at work within us,
(Ephesians 3:20 NIV)

3/21
Blessed is the one whose transgressions are forgiven, whose sins are covered.
(Psalm 32:1 NIV)

3/22
Because of the Lord's great love we are not consumed, for his compassions never fail.
(Lamentations 3:22 NIV)

3/23
Whatever you do, work at it with all your heart, as working for the Lord, not for human masters, (**Colossians 3:23** NIV)

3/24
"He is the Rock; his deeds are perfect. Everything he does is just and fair. He is a faithful God who does no wrong; how just and upright he is!"
(**Deuteronomy 32:4** NLT)

3/25
The Lord is good to those whose hope is in him, to the one who seeks him;
(**Lamentations 3:25** NIV)

3/26
For you are all children of God through faith in Christ Jesus.
(**Galatians 3:26** NLT)

3/27
And all who have been united with Christ in baptism have put on Christ, like putting on new clothes.
(**Galatians 3:27** NLT)

3/28
The Lord says, "I will guide you along the best pathway for your life. I will advise you and watch over you.
(**Psalms 32:8** NLT)

3/29
And now that you belong to Christ, you are the true children of Abraham. You are his heirs, and God's promise to Abraham belongs to you.
(**Galatians 3:29** NLT)

3/30
He must become greater and greater, and I must become less and less.
(**John 3:30** NLT)

3/31
Let the godly sing for joy to the lord; it is fitting for the pure to praise him.
(**Psalms 33:1** NLT)

April

4/1
Therefore I, a prisoner for serving the Lord, beg you to lead a life worthy of your calling, for you have been called by God.
(**Ephesians 4:1** NLT)

4/2
Preach the word; be prepared in season and out of season; correct, rebuke and encourage—with great patience and careful instruction.
(**2 Timothy 4:2** NIV)

4/3
Make every effort to keep yourselves united in the Spirit, binding yourselves together with peace.
(**Ephesians 4:3** NLT)

4/4
ALWAYS be full of joy in the Lord. I say it again—rejoice!
(**Philippians 4:4** NLT)

4/5
But you should keep a clear mind in every situation. Don't be afraid of suffering for the Lord. Work at telling others the Good News, and fully carry out the ministry God has given you.
(**2 Timothy 4:5** NLT)

4/6
Don't worry about anything; instead, pray about everything. Tell God what you need, and thank him for all he has done.
(**Philippians 4:6** NLT)

4/7
Submit yourselves, then, to God. Resist the devil, and he will flee from you.
(**James 4:7** NIV)

4/8
Finally, brothers and sisters, whatever is true, whatever is noble, whatever is right, whatever is pure, whatever is lovely, whatever is admirable—if anything is excellent or praiseworthy—think about such things.
(**Philippians 4:8** NIV)

4/9
We are hunted down, but never abandoned by God. We get knocked down, but we are not destroyed.
(**2 Corinthians 4:9** NLT)

4/10
Humble yourselves before the Lord, and he will lift you up.
(James 4:10 NIV)

4/11
Do you have the gift of speaking? Then speak as though God himself were speaking through you. Do you have the gift of helping others? Do it with all the strength and energy that God supplies. Then everything you do will bring glory to God through Jesus Christ. All glory and power to him forever and ever! Amen.
(1 Peter 4:11 NLT)

4/12
Don't let anyone look down on you because you are young, but set an example for the believers in speech, in conduct, in love, in faith and in purity.
(1 Timothy 4:12 NIV)

4/13
For I can do everything through Christ, who gives me strength.
(Philippians 4:13 NLT)

4/14
So then, since we have a great High Priest who has entered heaven, Jesus the Son of God, let us hold firmly to what we believe.
(Hebrews 4:14 NLT)

4/15
For we do not have a high priest who is unable to empathize with our weaknesses, but we have one who has been tempted in every way, just as we are—yet he did not sin.
(Hebrews 4:15 NIV)

4/16
So let us come boldly to the throne of our gracious God. There we will receive his mercy, and we will find grace to help us when we need it most.
(Hebrews 4:16 NLT)

4/17
For our light and momentary troubles are achieving for us an eternal glory that far outweighs them all.
(2 **Corinthians 4:17** NIV)

4/18
There is no fear in love. But perfect love drives out fear, because fear has to do with punishment. The one who fears is not made perfect in love.
(1 **John 4:18** NIV)

4/19
And this same God who takes care of me will supply all your needs from his glorious riches, which have been given to us in Christ Jesus.
(**Philippians 4:19** NLT)

4/20
Others, like seed sown on good soil, hear the word, accept it, and produce a crop—some thirty, some sixty, some a hundred times what was sown."
(**Mark 4:20** NIV)

4/21
As the deer pants for streams of water, so my soul pants for you, my God.
(**Psalm 42:1** NIV)

4/22
"I know that you can do anything, and no one can stop you.
(**Job 42:2** NLT)

4/23
Above all else, guard your heart, for everything you do flows from it.
(**Proverbs 4:23** NIV)

4/24
and to put on the new self, created to be like God in true righteousness and holiness.
(**Ephesians 4:24** NIV)

4/25
Why, my soul, are you downcast? Why so disturbed within me? Put your hope in God, for I will yet praise him, my Savior and my God.
(**Psalm 42:5** NIV)

4/26
"Give careful thought to the paths for your feet and be steadfast in all your ways."
(**Proverbs 4:26** NIV)

4:27
"You will open the eyes of the blind. You will free the captives from prison, releasing those who sit in dark dungeons."
(**Isaiah 42:7** NLT)

4/28
But each day the LORD pours his unfailing love upon me, and through each night I sing his songs, praying to God who gives me life.
(**Psalms 42:8** NLT)

4/29
"But from there you will seek the Lord your God and you will find him, if you search after him with all your heart and with all your soul."
(**Deuteronomy 4:29** ESV)

4/30
Even youths grow tired and weary, and young men stumble and fall; but those who hope in the Lord will renew their strength. They will soar on wings like eagles; they will run and not grow weary, they will walk and not be faint.
(**Isaiah 40:30**, 31 NIV)

May

5/1
Imitate God, therefore, in everything you do, because you are his dear children.
(**Ephesians 5:1** NLT)

5/2
and walk in the way of love, just as Christ loved us and gave himself up for us as a fragrant offering and sacrifice to God.
(**Ephesians 5:2** NIV)

5/3
"God blesses those who are poor and realize their need for him, for the Kingdom of Heaven is theirs.
(**Matthew 5:3**)

5/4
"For every child of God defeats this evil world, and we achieve this victory through our faith."
(1 **John 5:4** NLT)

Hope in Numbers

5/5
And who can win this battle against the world? Only those who believe that Jesus is the Son of God.
(1 **John 5:5** NLT)

5/6
Humble yourselves, therefore, under God's mighty hand, that he may lift you up in due time.
(1 **Peter 5:6** NIV)

5/7
Cast all your anxiety on him because he cares for you.
(1 **Peter 5:7** NIV)

5/8
For once you were full of darkness, but now you have light from the Lord. So live as people of light!
(**Ephesians 5:8** NLT)

5/9
Stand firm against him, and be strong in your faith. Remember that your family of believers all over the world is going through the same kind of suffering you are.
(1 **Peter 5:9** NLT)

5/10
In his kindness God called you to share in his eternal glory by means of Christ Jesus. So after you have suffered a little while, he will restore, support, and strengthen you, and he will place you on a firm foundation.
(1 **Peter 5:10** NLT)

5/11
But let all who take refuge in you rejoice; let them sing joyful praises forever. Spread your protection over them, that all who love your name may be filled with joy.
(**Psalms 5:11** NLT)

5/12
For you bless the godly, O Lord; you surround them with your shield of love.
(**Psalms 5:12** NLT)

5/13
You, my brothers and sisters, were called to be free. But do not use your freedom to indulge the flesh; rather, serve one another humbly in love.
(**Galatians 5:13** NIV)

5/14
"You are the light of the world—like a city on a hilltop that cannot be hidden.
(**Matthew 5:14** NLT)

5/15
He died for everyone so that those who receive his new life will no longer live for themselves. Instead, they will live for Christ, who died and was raised for them.
(2 **Corinthians 5:15** NLT)

5/16
Therefore confess your sins to each other and pray for each other so that you may be healed. The prayer of a righteous person is powerful and effective.
(**James 5:16** NIV)

5/17
This means that anyone who belongs to Christ has become a new person. The old life is gone; a new life has begun!
(2 **Corinthians 5:17** NLT)

5/18
Be thankful in all circumstances, for this is God's will for you who belong to Christ Jesus.
(1 **Thessalonians 5:18** NLT)

5/19
that God was reconciling the world to himself in Christ, not counting people's sins against them. And he has committed to us the message of reconciliation.
(2 **Corinthians 5:19** NIV)

5/20
So we are Christ's ambassadors; God is making his appeal through us. We speak for Christ when we plead, "Come back to God!"
(2 **Corinthians 5:20** NLT)

5/21
God made him who had no sin to be sin for us, so that in him we might become the righteousness of God.
(2 **Corinthians 5:21** NIV)

5/22
But the Holy Spirit produces this kind of fruit in our lives: love, joy, peace, patience, kindness, goodness, faithfulness, gentleness, and self-control. There is no law against these things!
(**Galatians 5:22**, 23 NLT)

5/23
Now may the God of peace make you holy in every way, and may your whole spirit and soul and body be kept blameless until our Lord Jesus Christ comes again.
(1 **Thessalonians 5:23** NLT)

5/24
The one who calls you is faithful, and he will do it.
(1 **Thessalonians 5:24** NLT)

5/25
Since we are living by the Spirit, let us follow the Spirit's leading in every part of our lives.
(**Galatians 5:25** NLT)

5/26
But I will reveal my name to my people, and they will come to know its power. Then at last they will recognize that I am the one who speaks to them."
(**Isaiah 52:6** NLT)

5/27
How beautiful on the mountains are the feet of the messenger who brings good news, the good news of peace and salvation, the news that the God of Israel reigns!
(**Isaiah 52:7** NLT)

5/28
But I am like an olive tree flourishing in the house of God; I trust in God's unfailing love for ever and ever.
(**Psalm 52:8** NIV)

5/29
For what you have done I will always praise you in the presence of your faithful people. And I will hope in your name, for your name is good.
(**Psalm 52:9** NIV)

5/30
I can do nothing on my own. I judge as God tells me. Therefore, my judgment is just, because I carry out the will of the one who sent me, not my own will.
(**John 5:30** NLT)

5/31
Jesus answered them, "It is not the healthy who need a doctor, but the sick.
(**Luke 5:31** NIV)

June

6/1
So let us stop going over the basic teachings about Christ again and again. Let us go on instead and become mature in our understanding. Surely we don't need to start again with the fundamental importance of repenting from evil deeds and placing our faith in God.
(**Hebrews 6:1** NLT)

6/2
Carry each other's burdens, and in this way you will fulfill the law of Christ.
(**Galatians 6:2** NIV)

6/3
We live in such a way that no one will stumble because of us, and no one will find fault with our ministry.
(2 **Corinthians 6:3** NLT)

6/4
For we died and were buried with Christ by baptism. And just as Christ was raised from the dead by the glorious power of the Father, now we also may live new lives.
(**Romans 6:4** NLT)

6/5
And you must love the Lord your God with all your heart, all your soul, and all your strength. (**Deuteronomy 6:5** NLT)

6/6
But godliness with contentment is great gain.
(1 **Timothy 6:6** NIV)

6/7
Do not be deceived: God cannot be mocked. A man reaps what he sows.
(**Galatians 6:7** NIV)

6/8
"He has shown you, O mortal, what is good. And what does the LORD require of you? To act justly and to love mercy and to walk humbly with your God."
(**Micah 6:8** NIV)

6/9
So let's not get tired of doing what is good. At just the right time we will reap a harvest of blessing if we don't give up.
(**Galatians 6:9** NLT)

6/10
"For God is not unjust. He will not forget how hard you have worked for him and how you have shown your love to him by caring for other believers, as you still do."
(**Hebrews 6:10** NLT)

6/11
"Put on the full armor of God, so that you can take your stand against the devil's schemes."
(**Ephesians 6:11** NIV)

6/12
Fight the good fight of the faith. Take hold of the eternal life to which you were called when you made your good confession in the presence of many witnesses.
(1 **Timothy 6:12** NIV)

6/13
"To all who mourn in Israel, he will give a crown of beauty for ashes, a joyous blessing instead of mourning, festive praise instead of despair. In their righteousness, they will be like great oaks that the LORD has planted for his own glory."
(**Isaiah 61:3** NLT)

6/14
For sin shall no longer be your master, because you are not under the law, but under grace.
(**Romans 6:14** NIV)

6/15
For you have heard my vows, O God. You have given me an inheritance reserved for those who fear your name.
(**Psalms 61:5** NLT)

6/16
This is what the Lord says: "Stop at the crossroads and look around. Ask for the old, godly way, and walk in it. Travel its path, and you will find rest for your souls.
(**Jeremiah 6:16a** NLT)

6/17
Instead of shame and dishonor, you will enjoy a double share of honor. You will possess a double portion of prosperity in your land, and everlasting joy will be yours.
(**Isaiah 61:7** NLT)

6/18
"So God has given both his promise and his oath. These two things are unchangeable because it is impossible for God to lie. Therefore, we who have fled to him for refuge can have great confidence as we hold to the hope that lies before us."
(**Hebrews 6:18** NLT)

6/19
This hope is a strong and trustworthy anchor for our souls. It leads us through the curtain into God's inner sanctuary.
(**Hebrews 6:19** NLT)

6/20
Store your treasures in heaven, where moths and rust cannot destroy, and thieves do not break in and steal.
(**Matthew 6:20** NLT)

6/21
For where your treasure is, there your heart will be also.
(**Matthew 6:21** NIV)

6/22
He alone is my rock and my salvation, my fortress where I will never be shaken.
(**Psalms 62:2** NLT)

6/23
For the wages of sin is death, but the free gift of God is eternal life through Christ Jesus our Lord.
(**Romans 6:23** NLT)

6/24
"The Lord bless you and keep you; the Lord make his face shine on you and be gracious to you; the Lord turn his face toward you and give you peace." '
(**Numbers 6:24**-26 NIV)

6/25
Yes, my soul, find rest in God; my hope comes from him.
(**Psalm 62:5** NIV)

6/26
He alone is my rock and my salvation, my fortress where I will not be shaken.
(**Psalms 62:6** NLT)

6/27
My salvation and my honor depend on God; he is my mighty rock, my refuge.
(**Psalm 62:7** NIV)

6/28
Trust in him at all times, you people; pour out your hearts to him, for God is our refuge.
(**Ptsalm 62:8** NIV)

6/29
""Yet I tell you that not even Solomon in all his splendor was dressed like one of these."
(Matthew 6:29 NIV)

6/30
"And if God cares so wonderfully for wildflowers that are here today and thrown into the fire tomorrow, he will certainly care for you. Why do you have so little faith?"
(**Matthew 6:30** NLT)

July

7/1
Therefore, since we have these promises, dear friends, let us purify ourselves from everything that contaminates body and spirit, perfecting holiness out of reverence for God.
(**2 Corinthians 7:1** NIV)

7/2
Obey my commands and live! Guard my instructions as you guard your own eyes.
(**Proverbs 7:2** NLT)

7/3
Tie them on your fingers as a reminder. Write them deep within your heart.
(**Proverbs 7:3** NLT)

7/4
But may all who search for you be filled with joy and gladness in you. May those who love your salvation repeatedly shout, "God is great!"
(**Psalms 70:4** NLT)

7/5
Better to be criticized by a wise person than to be praised by a fool.
(**Ecclesiastes 7:5** NLT)

7/6
"But God, who encourages those who are discouraged, encouraged us by the arrival of Titus."
(**2 Corinthians 7:6** NLT)

7/7
"Ask and it will be given to you; seek and you will find; knock and the door will be opened to you. (**Matthew 7:7** NIV)

7/8
"For everyone who asks receives; the one who seeks finds; and to the one who knocks, the door will be opened."(**Matthew 7:8** NIV)

7/9
If you do not stand firm in your faith, you will not stand at all.' "
(**Isaiah 7:9**b NIV)

7/10
God is my shield, saving those whose hearts are true and right.
(**Psalms 7:10** NLT)

7/11
"So if you sinful people know how to give good gifts to your children, how much more will your heavenly Father give good gifts to those who ask him."
(**Matthew 7:11** NLT)

7/12
"Do to others whatever you would like them to do to you. This is the essence of all that is taught in the law and the prophets.
(**Matthew 7:12** NLT)

7/13
Be my rock of refuge, to which I can always go; give the command to save me, for you are my rock and my fortress.
(**Psalm 71:3** NIV)

7/14
Then if my people who are called by my name will humble themselves and pray and seek my face and turn from their wicked ways, I will hear from heaven and will forgive their sins and restore their land.
(2 **Chronicles 7:14** NLT)

7/15
For you have been my hope, Sovereign Lord, my confidence since my youth.
(**Psalm 71:5** NIV)

7/16
Yes, you have been with me from birth; from my mother's womb you have cared for me. No wonder I am always praising you!
(**Psalms 71:6** NLT)

7/17
My life is an example to many, because you have been my strength and protection.
(**Psalms 71:7** NLT)

7/18
Who is a God like you, who pardons sin and forgives the transgression of the remnant of his inheritance? You do not stay angry forever but delight to show mercy.
(**Micah 7:18** NIV)

7/19
For the law never made anything perfect. But now we have confidence in a better hope, through which we draw near to God.
(Hebrews 7:19 NLT)

7/20
You will show us your faithfulness and unfailing love as you promised to our ancestors Abraham and Jacob long ago.
(Micah 7:20 NLT)

7/21
"No, do not be afraid of those nations, for the LORD your God is among you, and he is a great and awesome God.
(Deuteronomy 7:21 NLT)

7/22
I love God's law with all my heart.
(Romans 7:22 NLT)

7/23
God paid a high price for you, so don't be enslaved by the world.
(1 **Corinthians 7:23** NLT)

7/24
"Therefore everyone who hears these words of mine and puts them into practice is like a wise man who built his house on the rock. The rain came down, the streams rose, and the winds blew and beat against that house; yet it did not fall, because it had its foundation on the rock."
(Matthew 7:24-25 NIV)

7/25
What a wretched man I am! Who will rescue me from this body that is subject to death? Thanks be to God, who delivers me through Jesus Christ our Lord!
(Romans 7:24, **25**a NIV)

7/26
He is the kind of high priest we need because he is holy and blameless, unstained by sin. He has been set apart from sinners and has been given the highest place of honor in heaven.
(Hebrews 7:26 NLT)

Hope in Numbers

7/27
Then the sovereignty, power and greatness of all the kingdoms under heaven will be handed over to the holy people of the Most High. His kingdom will be an everlasting kingdom, and all rulers will worship and obey him.'
(**Daniel 7:27** NIV)

7/28
For you are God, O Sovereign Lord. Your words are truth, and you have promised these good things to your servant.
(2 **Samuel 7:28** NLT)

7/29
And now, may it please you to bless the house of your servant, so that it may continue forever before you. For you have spoken, and when you grant a blessing to your servant, O Sovereign Lord, it is an eternal blessing!"
(2 **Samuel 7:29** NLT)

7/30
My flesh and my heart may fail, but God is the strength of my heart and my portion forever.
(**Psalms 73**:26 NIV)

7/31
Surely God is good to Israel, to those who are pure in heart.
(**Psalm 73:1** NIV)

August

8/1
Therefore, there is now no condemnation for those who are in Christ Jesus,
(**Romans 8:1** NIV)

8/2
And because you belong to him, the power of the life-giving Spirit has freed you from the power of sin that leads to death.
(**Romans 8:2** NLT)

8/3
But the person who loves God is the one whom God recognizes.
(1 **Corinthians 8:3** NLT)

8/4
"But the believers who were scattered preached the Good News about Jesus wherever they went."
(**Acts 8:4** NLT)

8/5
Those who live according to the flesh have their minds set on what the flesh desires; but those who live in accordance with the Spirit have their minds set on what the Spirit desires.
(**Romans 8:5** NIV)

8/6
But for us, There is one God, the Father, by whom all things were created, and for whom we live. And there is one Lord, Jesus Christ, through whom all things were created, and through whom we live.
(1 **Corinthians 8:6** NLT)

8/7
"And though you started with little, you will end with much."
(**Job 8:7** NLT)

8/8
Still other seed fell on good soil. It came up and yielded a crop, a hundred times more than was sown." When he said this, he called out, "Whoever has ears to hear, let them hear."
(**Luke 8:8** NIV)

8/9
But you are not controlled by your sinful nature. You are controlled by the Spirit if you have the Spirit of God living in you. (And remember that those who do not have the Spirit of Christ living in them do not belong to him at all.)
(**Romans 8:9** NLT)

8/10
Nehemiah said, "Go and enjoy choice food and sweet drinks, and send some to those who have nothing prepared. This day is holy to our Lord. Do not grieve, for the joy of the Lord is your strength."
(**Nehemiah 8:10** NIV)

8/11
The Spirit of God, who raised Jesus from the dead, lives in you. And just as God raised Christ Jesus from the dead, he will give life to your mortal bodies by this same Spirit living within you.
(**Romans 8:11** NLT)

Hope in Numbers

8/12
When Jesus spoke again to the people, he said, "I am the light of the world. Whoever follows me will never walk in darkness, but will have the light of life."
(**John 8:12** NIV)

8/13
Make the Lord of Heaven's Armies holy in your life. He is the one you should fear. He is the one who should make you tremble.
(**Isaiah 8:13** NLT)

8/14
For all who are led by the Spirit of God are children of God.
(**Romans 8:14** NLT)

8/15
And the seeds that fell on the good soil represent honest, good-hearted people who hear God's word, cling to it, and patiently produce a huge harvest.
(**Luke 8:15** NLT)

8/16
"No one lights a lamp and then covers it with a bowl or hides it under a bed. A lamp is placed on a stand, where its light can be seen by all who enter the house.
(**Luke 8:16** NLT)

8/17
"I love all who love me. Those who search will surely find me.
(**Proverbs 8:17** NLT)

8/18
Yet what we suffer now is nothing compared to the glory he will reveal to us later.
(**Romans 8:18** NLT)

8/19
For all creation is waiting eagerly for that future day when God will reveal who his children really are.
(**Romans 8:19** NLT)

8/20
"But look, God will not reject a person of integrity, nor will he lend a hand to the wicked.
(**Job 8:20** NLT)

Birthday Bible Verses / Verse of the Day

8/21
We are careful to be honorable before the Lord, but we also want everyone else to see that we are honorable.
(**2 Corinthians 8:21** NLT)

8/22
"The LORD formed me from the beginning, before he created anything else.
(**Proverbs 8:22** NLT)

8/23
and he prayed, "O Lord, God of Israel, there is no God like you in all of heaven above or on the earth below. You keep your covenant and show unfailing love to all who walk before you in wholehearted devotion.
(1 **Kings 8:23** NLT)

8/24
We were given this hope when we were saved. (If we already have something, we don't need to hope for it.
(**Romans 8:24** NLT)

8/25
But if we look forward to something we don't yet have, we must wait patiently and confidently.
(**Romans 8:25** NLT)

8/26
And the Holy Spirit helps us in our weakness. For example, we don't know what God wants us to pray for. But the Holy Spirit prays for us with groanings that cannot be expressed in words.
(**Romans 8:26** NLT)

8/27
And the Father who knows all hearts knows what the Spirit is saying, for the Spirit pleads for us believers in harmony with God's own will.
(**Romans 8:27** NLT)

8/28
And we know that in all things God works for the good of those who love him, who have been called according to his purpose.
(**Romans 8:28** NIV)

8/29
And the one who sent me is with me—he has not deserted me. For I always do what pleases him."
(**John 8:29** NLT)

213

8/30
Then I was constantly at his side. I was filled with delight day after day, rejoicing always in his presence,
(**Proverbs 8:30** NIV)

8/31
What, then, shall we say in response to these things? If God is for us, who can be against us?
(**Romans 8:31** NIV)

September

9/1
I will praise you, Lord, with all my heart; I will tell of all the marvelous things you have done.
(**Psalms 9:1** NLT)

9/2
I will be filled with joy because of you. I will sing praises to your name, O Most High.
(**Psalms 9:2** NLT)

9/3
The Lord said to him, "I have heard your prayer and your petition. I have set this Temple apart to be holy—this place you have built where my name will be honored forever. I will always watch over it, for it is dear to my heart.
(1 **Kings 9:3** NLT)

9/4
I prayed to the Lord my God and confessed: "O Lord, you are a great and awesome God! You always fulfill your covenant and keep your promises of unfailing love to those who love you and obey your commands.
(**Daniel 9:4** NLT)

9/5
But while I am here in the world, I am the light of the world."
(**John 9:5** NLT)

9/6
"For a child is born to us, a son is given to us. The government will rest on his shoulders. And he will be called: Wonderful Counselor, Mighty God, Everlasting Father, Prince of Peace."
(**Isaiah 9:6** NLT)

9/7
You must each decide in your heart how much to give. And don't give reluctantly or in response to pressure. "For God loves a person who gives cheerfully."
(2 **Corinthians 9:7** NLT)

9/8
So don't bother correcting mockers; they will only hate you. But correct the wise, and they will love you.
(**Proverbs 9:8** NLT)

9/9
But the Lord our God is merciful and forgiving, even though we have rebelled against him.
(**Daniel 9:9** NLT)

9/10
Those who know your name trust in you, for you, Lord, have never forsaken those who seek you.
(**Psalm 9:10** NIV)

9/11
Those who live in the shelter of the Most High will find rest in the shadow of the Almighty.
(**Psalms 91:1** NLT)

9/12
This I declare about the Lord : He alone is my refuge, my place of safety; he is my God, and I trust him.
(**Psalms 91:2** NLT)

9/13
For he will rescue you from every trap and protect you from deadly disease.
(**Psalms 91:3** NLT)

9/14
He will cover you with his feathers. He will shelter you with his wings. His faithful promises are your armor and protection.
(**Psalms 91:4** NLT)

9/15
Thank God for this gift too wonderful for words!
(2 **Corinthians 9:15** NLT)

9/16
"But I have raised you up for this very purpose, that I might show you my power and that my name might be proclaimed in all the earth."
(**Exodus 9:16** NIV)

9/17
 But you are a God of forgiveness, gracious and merciful, slow to become angry, and rich in unfailing love. You did not abandon them,
(**Nehemiah 9:17** NLTb)

9/18
But God will never forget the needy; the hope of the afflicted will never perish.
(**Psalm 9:18** NIV)

9/19
Lord, listen! Lord, forgive! Lord, hear and act! For your sake, my God, do not delay, because your city and your people bear your Name."
(**Daniel 9:19** NIV)

9/20
To the Jews I became like a Jew, to win the Jews. To those under the law I became like one under the law (though I myself am not under the law), so as to win those under the law.
(1 **Corinthians 9:20** NIV)

9/21
To those not having the law I became like one not having the law (though I am not free from God's law but am under Christ's law), so as to win those not having the law.
(1 **Corinthians 9:21** NIV)

9/22
When I am with those who are weak, I share their weakness, for I want to bring the weak to Christ. Yes, I try to find common ground with everyone, doing everything I can to save some.
 (1 **Corinthians 9:22** NLT)

9/23
"What do you mean, 'If I can'?" Jesus asked. "Anything is possible if a person believes."
(**Mark 9:23** NLT)

9/24
Don't you realize that in a race everyone runs, but only one person gets the prize? So run to win!
(1 **Corinthians 9:24** NLT)

9/25
All athletes are disciplined in their training. They do it to win a prize that will fade away, but we do it for an eternal prize.
(1 **Corinthians 9:25** NLT)

9/26
Therefore I do not run like someone running aimlessly; I do not fight like a boxer beating the air.
(1 **Corinthians 9:26** NIV)

9/27
No, I strike a blow to my body and make it my slave so that after I have preached to others, I myself will not be disqualified for the prize.
(1 **Corinthians 9:27** NIV)

9/28
so also Christ died once for all time as a sacrifice to take away the sins of many people. He will come again, not to deal with our sins, but to bring salvation to all who are eagerly waiting for him.
(**Hebrews 9:28** NLT)

9/29
Then he touched their eyes and said, "Because of your faith, it will happen."
(**Matthew 9:29** NLT)

9/30
What then shall we say? That the Gentiles, who did not pursue righteousness, have obtained it, a righteousness that is by faith;
(**Romans 9:30** NIV)

October

10/1
Dear brothers and sisters, the longing of my heart and my prayer to God is for the people of Israel to be saved.
(**Romans 10:1** NLT)

10/2
He told them, "The harvest is plentiful, but the workers are few. Ask the Lord of the harvest, therefore, to send out workers into his harvest field.
(**Luke 10:2** NIV)

10/3
Go! I am sending you out like lambs among wolves.
(**Luke 10:3** NIV)

10/4
Rise up; this matter is in your hands. We will support you, so take courage and do it."
(**Ezra 10:4** NIV)

10/5
We destroy every proud obstacle that keeps people from knowing God. We capture their rebellious thoughts and teach them to obey Christ.
(2 **Corinthians 10:5** NLT)

10/6
"No one is like you, Lord; you are great, and your name is mighty in power."
(**Jeremiah 10:6** NIV).

10/7
We have happy memories of the godly, but the name of a wicked person rots away.
(**Proverbs 10:7** NLT)

10/8
"I may seem to be boasting too much about the authority given to us by the Lord. But our authority builds you up; it doesn't tear you down. So I will not be ashamed of using my authority."
(2 **Corinthians 10:8** NLT)

10/9
If you confess with your mouth that Jesus is Lord and believe in your heart that God raised him from the dead, you will be saved.
(**Romans 10:9** NLT)

10/10
The thief comes only to steal and kill and destroy; I have come that they may have life, and have it to the full.
(**John 10:10** NIV)

10/11
As the Scriptures tell us, "Anyone who trusts in him will never be disgraced."
(**Romans 10:11** NLT)

10/12
Be strong, and let us fight bravely for our people and the cities of our God. The Lord will do what is good in his sight."
(2 **Samuel 10:12** NIV)

10/13
No temptation has overtaken you except what is common to mankind. And God is faithful; he will not let you be tempted beyond what you can bear. But when you are tempted, he will also provide a way out so that you can endure it.
(1 **Corinthians 10:13** NIV)

10/14
But you, God, see the trouble of the afflicted; you consider their grief and take it in hand. The victims commit themselves to you; you are the helper of the fatherless.
(**Psalm 10:14** NIV)

10/15
And how will anyone go and tell them without being sent? That is why the Scriptures say, "How beautiful are the feet of messengers who bring good news.
(**Romans 10:15** NLT)

10/16
"This is the new covenant I will make with my people on that day, says the Lord : I will put my laws in their hearts, and I will write them on their minds."
(**Hebrews 10:16** NLT)

10/17
""For the LORD your God is the God of gods and Lord of lords. He is the great God, the mighty and awesome God, who shows no partiality and cannot be bribed."
(**Deuteronomy 10:17** NLT)

10/18
No one can take my life from me. I sacrifice it voluntarily. For I have the authority to lay it down when I want to and also to take it up again. For this is what my Father has commanded."
(**John 10:18** NLT)

10/19
"Don't be afraid," he said, "for you are very precious to God. Peace! Be encouraged! Be strong!" As he spoke these words to me, I suddenly felt stronger and said to him, "Please speak to me, my lord, for you have strengthened me."
(**Daniel 10:19** NLT)

10/20
You must fear the Lord your God and worship him and cling to him. Your oaths must be in his name alone.
(**Deuteronomy 10:20** NLT)

10/21
Lord, hear my prayer! Listen to my plea!
(**Psalms 102:1** NLT)

10/22
let us draw near to God with a sincere heart and with the full assurance that faith brings, having our hearts sprinkled to cleanse us from a guilty conscience and having our bodies washed with pure water.
(**Hebrews 10:22** NIV)

10/23
Let us hold tightly without wavering to the hope we affirm, for God can be trusted to keep his promise.
(**Hebrews 10:23** NLT)

10/24
Let us think of ways to motivate one another to acts of love and good works.
(**Hebrews 10:24** NLT)

10/25
And let us not neglect our meeting together, as some people do, but encourage one another, especially now that the day of his return is drawing near.
(**Hebrews 10:25** NLT)

10/26
For "the earth is the lord's, and everything in it."
(1 **Corinthians 10:26** NLT)

10/27
Jesus looked at them intently and said, "Humanly speaking, it is impossible. But not with God. Everything is possible with God."
(**Mark 10:27** NLT)

10/28
"Don't be afraid of those who want to kill your body; they cannot touch your soul. Fear only God, who can destroy both soul and body in hell.
(Matthew 10:28 NLT)

10/29
The way of the lord is a stronghold to those with integrity, but it destroys the wicked.
(Proverbs 10:29 NLT)

10/30
And the very hairs on your head are all numbered.
(Matthew 10:30 NLT)

10/31
So whether you eat or drink, or whatever you do, do it all for the glory of God.
(1 **Corinthians 10:31** NLT)

November

11/1
Now faith is confidence in what we hope for and assurance about what we do not see.
(Hebrews 11:1 NIV)

11/2
Pride leads to disgrace, but with humility comes wisdom.
(Proverbs 11:2 NLT)

11/3
But there is one thing I want you to know: The head of every man is Christ, the head of woman is man, and the head of Christ is God.
(1 **Corinthians 11:3** NLT)

11/4
If you wait for perfect conditions, you will never get anything done
(Ecclesiastes 11:4 TLB)

11/5
He will wear righteousness like a belt and truth like an undergarment.
(Isaiah 11:5 NLT)

11/6
And it is impossible to please God without faith. Anyone who wants to come to him must believe that God exists and that he rewards those who sincerely seek him.
(**Hebrews 11:6** NLT)

11/7
For the Lord is righteous, he loves justice; the upright will see his face.
(**Psalm 11:7** NIV)

11/8
The godly are rescued from trouble, and it falls on the wicked instead.
(**Proverbs 11:8** NLT)

11/9
Young people, it's wonderful to be young! Enjoy every minute of it. Do everything you want to do; take it all in. But remember that you must give an account to God for everything you do.
(**Ecclesiastes 11:9** NLT)

11/10
For everyone who asks receives; the one who seeks finds; and to the one who knocks, the door will be opened.
(**Luke 11:10** NIV)

11/11
Praise the lord ! I will thank the lord with all my heart as I meet with his godly people.
(**Psalms 111:1** NLT)

11/12
How amazing are the deeds of the lord ! All who delight in him should ponder them.
(**Psalms 111:2** NLT)

11/13
So if you sinful people know how to give good gifts to your children, how much more will your heavenly Father give the Holy Spirit to those who ask him."
(**Luke 11:13** NLT)

11/14
He causes us to remember his wonderful works. How gracious and merciful is our lord !
(**Psalms 111:4** NLT)

11/15
For since their rejection meant that God offered salvation to the rest of the world, their acceptance will be even more wonderful. It will be life for those who were dead!
(Romans 11:15 NLT)

11/16
"But be careful. Don't let your heart be deceived so that you turn away from the lord and serve and worship other gods.
(Deuteronomy 11:16 NLT)

11/17
All he does is just and good, and all his commandments are trustworthy.
(Psalms 111:7 NLT)

11/18
For the message of the cross is foolishness to those who are perishing, but to us who are being saved it is the power of God.
(1 Corinthians 1:18 NIV

11/19
Cling to your faith in Christ, and keep your conscience clear. For some people have deliberately violated their consciences; as a result, their faith has been shipwrecked.
(1 Timothy 1:19 NLT)

11/20
But you, Lord Almighty, who judge righteously and test the heart and mind, let me see your vengeance on them, for to you I have committed my cause.
(Jeremiah 11:20 NIV)

11/21
Praise the lord ! How joyful are those who fear the lord and delight in obeying his commands.
(Psalms 112:1 NLT)

11/22
"Be careful to obey all these commands I am giving you. Show love to the lord your God by walking in his ways and holding tightly to him.
(Deuteronomy 11:22 NLT)

11/23
I tell you the truth, you can say to this mountain, 'May you be lifted up and thrown into the sea,' and it will happen. But you must really believe it will happen and have no doubt in your heart.
(**Mark 11:2**3 NLT)

11/24
Light shines in the darkness for the godly. They are generous, compassionate, and righteous.
(**Psalms 112:4** NLT)

11/25
The generous will prosper; those who refresh others will themselves be refreshed.
 (**Proverbs 11:25** NLT)

11/26
Surely the righteous will never be shaken; they will be remembered forever.
(**Psalm 112:6** NIV)

11/27
They do not fear bad news; they confidently trust the lord to care for them.
(**Psalms 112:7** NLT)

11/28
Then Jesus said, "Come to me, all of you who are weary and carry heavy burdens, and I will give you rest.
(**Matthew 11:28** NLT)

11/29
Take my yoke upon you. Let me teach you, because I am humble and gentle at heart, and you will find rest for your souls.
(**Matthew 11:29** NLT)

11/30
The seeds of good deeds become a tree of life; a wise person wins friends.
(**Proverbs 11:30** NLT)

December

12/1
"Therefore, since we are surrounded by such a huge crowd of witnesses to the life of faith, let us strip off every weight that slows us down, especially the sin that so easily trips us up. And let us run with endurance the race God has set before us."
(**Hebrews 12:1** NLT)

12/2
Do not conform to the pattern of this world, but be transformed by the renewing of your mind. Then you will be able to test and approve what God's will is—his good, pleasing and perfect will.
(**Romans 12:2** NIV)

12/3
Those who are wise will shine as bright as the sky, and those who lead many to righteousness will shine like the stars forever.
(**Daniel 12:3** NLT)

12/4
In that day you will say: "Give praise to the Lord, proclaim his name; make known among the nations what he has done, and proclaim that his name is exalted.
(**Isaiah 12:4** NIV)

12/5
Sing to the Lord, for he has done glorious things; let this be known to all the world.
(**Isaiah 12:5** NIV)

12/6
So now, come back to your God. Act with love and justice, and always depend on him.
(**Hosea 12:6** NLT)

12/7
A spiritual gift is given to each of us so we can help each other.
(1 **Corinthians 12:7** NLT)

12/8
If your gift is to encourage others, be encouraging. If it is giving, give generously. If God has given you leadership ability, take the responsibility seriously. And if you have a gift for showing kindness to others, do it gladly.
(**Romans 12:8** NLT)

Hope in Numbers

12/9
Don't just pretend to love others. Really love them. Hate what is wrong. Hold tightly to what is good.
(**Romans 12:9** NLT)

12/10
Be devoted to one another in love. Honor one another above yourselves.
(**Romans 12:10** NIV)

12/11
"Never let the fire in your heart go out. Keep it alive. Serve the Lord."
(**Romans 12:11** NIRV)

12/12
Be joyful in hope, patient in affliction, faithful in prayer.
(**Romans 12:12** NIV)

12/13
That's the whole story. Here now is my final conclusion: Fear God and obey his commands, for this is everyone's duty.
(**Ecclesiastes 12:13** NLT)

12/14
Work at living in peace with everyone, and work at living a holy life, for those who are not holy will not see the Lord.
(**Hebrews 12:14** NLT)

12/15
Rejoice with those who rejoice; mourn with those who mourn.
(**Romans 12:15** NIV)

12/16
Live in harmony with one another. Do not be proud, but be willing to associate with people of low position. Do not be conceited.
(**Romans 12:16** NIV)

12/17
The lord keeps you from all harm and watches over your life.
(**Psalms 121:7** NLT)

12/18
Do all that you can to live in peace with everyone.
(**Romans 12:18** NLT)

12/19
Do not take revenge, my dear friends, but leave room for God's wrath, for it is written: "It is mine to avenge; I will repay," says the Lord.
(Romans 12:19 NIV)

12/20
""When the LORD your God expands your territory as he has promised, and you have the urge to eat meat, you may freely eat meat whenever you want."
(Deuteronomy 12:20 NLT)

12/21
"Yes, a person is a fool to store up earthly wealth but not have a rich relationship with God."
(Luke 12:21 NLT)

12/22
The lord will not abandon his people, because that would dishonor his great name. For it has pleased the lord to make you his very own people.
(1 **Samuel 12:22** NLT)

12/23
""As for me, I will certainly not sin against the LORD by ending my prayers for you. And I will continue to teach you what is good and right."
(1 **Samuel 12:23** NLT)

12/24
But be sure to fear the lord and faithfully serve him. Think of all the wonderful things he has done for you.
(1 **Samuel 12:24** NLT)

12/25
Those who love their life in this world will lose it. Those who care nothing for their life in this world will keep it for eternity.
(John 12:25 NLT)

12/26
"Pray for the peace of Jerusalem: "May those who love you be secure."
(Psalm 122:6 NIV)

12/27
"This means that all of creation will be shaken and removed, so that only unshakable things will remain."
(Hebrews 12:27 NLT)

12/28
Since we are receiving a Kingdom that is unshakable, let us be thankful and please God by worshiping him with holy fear and awe.
(**Hebrews 12:28** NLT)

12/29
for our "God is a consuming fire."
(**Hebrews 12:29** NIV)

12/30
And you must love the lord your God with all your heart, all your soul, all your mind, and all your strength.'
(**Mark 12:30** NLT)

12/31
"Seek the Kingdom of God above all else, and he will give you everything you need."
(**Luke 12:31** NLT)

JERSEY NUMBER BIBLE VERSES

#1st Commandment "No other gods"

#2nd Commandment "Thou shall not have any Idols before me"

#3rd Commandment "Thou shall not use the Lord's name in vain"

#4th Commandment "Remember to observe the Sabbath day by keeping it holy"

#5th Commandment 'Honor your father and mother"

#6th Commandment "You must not murder"

#7th Commandment "You must not commit adultery"

#8th Commandment "You must not steal"

#9th Commandment "You must not testify falsely against your neighbor"

#10th Commandment "Don't covet"

#11 = Psalm **1:1**-2 NIV
Blessed is the one who does not walk in step with the wicked or stand in the way that sinners take or sit in the company of mockers, but whose delight is in the law of the Lord, and who meditates on his law day and night.

#12 = James **1:2** NIV
Consider it pure joy, my brothers and sisters, whenever you face trials of many kinds,

#13 = Philippians **1:3** NLT
Every time I think of you, I give thanks to my God.

Hope in Numbers

#14 = 2 Corinthians **1:4** NLT
He comforts us in all our troubles so that we can comfort others. When they are troubled, we will be able to give them the same comfort God has given us.

#15 = James **1:5** NIV
If any of you lacks wisdom, you should ask God, who gives generously to all without finding fault, and it will be given to you.

#16 = Philippians **1:6** NIV
being confident of this, that he who began a good work in you will carry it on to completion until the day of Christ Jesus.

#17 = 2 Timothy **1:7** NLT
For God has not given us a spirit of fear and timidity, but of power, love, and self-discipline.

#18 = Joshua **1:8** NIV
Keep this Book of the Law always on your lips; meditate on it day and night, so that you may be careful to do everything written in it. Then you will be prosperous and successful.

#19 = Joshua **1:9** NIV
Have I not commanded you? Be strong and courageous. Do not be afraid; do not be discouraged, for the Lord your God will be with you wherever you go."

#20 = Psalms **20**:7 NLT
Some nations boast of their chariots and horses, but we boast in the name of the lord our God.

#21 = Hebrews **2:1** NLT
"So we must listen very carefully to the truth we have heard, or we may drift away from it."

#22 = Philippians **2:2** NL
Then make me truly happy by agreeing wholeheartedly with each other, loving one another, and working together with one mind and purpose.

#23 = Philippians **2:3** NLT
Don't be selfish; don't try to impress others. Be humble, thinking of others as better than yourselves.

#24 = Philippians **2:4** NLT
Don't look out only for your own interests, but take an interest in others, too.

#25 = Philippians **2:5** NLT
You must have the same attitude that Christ Jesus had.

#26 = 1 John **2:6** NLT
Those who say they live in God should live their lives as Jesus did.

#27 = Colossians **2:7** NLT
Let your roots grow down into him, and let your lives be built on him. Then your faith will grow strong in the truth you were taught, and you will overflow with thankfulness.

#28 = Ephesians **2:8** NIV
For it is by grace you have been saved, through faith—and this is not from yourselves, it is the gift of God

#29 = 1 Corinthians **2:9** NIV
However, as it is written: "What no eye has seen, what no ear has heard, and what no human mind has conceived" — the things God has prepared for those who love him—

#30 = Psalms **30**:5 NLT
For his anger lasts only a moment, but his favor lasts a lifetime! Weeping may last through the night, but joy comes with the morning.

#31 = Hebrews **3:1** NIV
Therefore, holy brothers and sisters, who share in the heavenly calling, fix your thoughts on Jesus, whom we acknowledge as our apostle and high priest.

#32 = Colossians **3:2** NIV
Set your minds on things above, not on earthly things.

#33 =Psalm **3:3** NIV
But you, Lord, are a shield around me, my glory, the One who lifts my head high.

#34 = Ecclesiastes **3:4** NIV
a time to weep and a time to laugh, a time to mourn and a time to dance,

#35 = Proverbs **3:5** NIV
Trust in the Lord with all your heart and lean not on your own understanding;

#36 = Proverbs **3:6** NLT
Seek his will in all you do, and he will show you which path to take.

#37 = Philippians **3:7** NLT
I once thought these things were valuable, but now I consider them worthless because of what Christ has done.

#38 = Matthew **3:8** NLT
Prove by the way you live that you have repented of your sins and turned to God.

#39 = 2 Peter **3:9** NIV
The Lord is not slow in keeping his promise, as some understand slowness. Instead he is patient with you, not wanting anyone to perish, but everyone to come to repentance.

#40 = Isaiah **40**:30-31 NIV
"Even youths grow tired and weary, and young men stumble and fall; but those who hope in the Lord will renew their strength. They will soar on wings like eagles; they will run and not grow weary, they will walk and not be faint."

#41 = Ephesians **4:1** NLT
Therefore I, a prisoner for serving the Lord, beg you to lead a life worthy of your calling, for you have been called by God.

#42 = 2 Timothy **4:2** NIV
Preach the word; be prepared in season and out of season; correct, rebuke and encourage—with great patience and careful instruction.

#43 = Ephesians **4:3** NLT
Make every effort to keep yourselves united in the Spirit, binding yourselves together with peace.

#44 = Philippians **4:4** NLT
ALWAYS be full of joy in the Lord. I say it again—rejoice!

#45 = 2 Timothy **4:5** NLT
But you should keep a clear mind in every situation. Don't be afraid of suffering for the Lord. Work at telling others the Good News, and fully carry out the ministry God has given you.

#46 = Philippians **4:6** NLT
Don't worry about anything; instead, pray about everything. Tell God what you need, and thank him for all he has done.

#47 = James **4:7** NIV
Submit yourselves, then, to God. Resist the devil, and he will flee from you.

#48 = 1 Timothy **4:8** NLT
"Physical training is good, but training for godliness is much better, promising benefits in this life and in the life to come."

#49 = Ecclesiastes **4:9** NLT
Two people are better off than one, for they can help each other succeed.

#50 = Genesis **50**:20 NLT
"You intended to harm me, but God intended it all for good. He brought me to this position so I could save the lives of many people."

#51 = Ephesians **5:1** NLT
Imitate God, therefore, in everything you do, because you are his dear children.

#52 = Ephesians **5:2** NIV
and walk in the way of love, just as Christ loved us and gave himself up for us as a fragrant offering and sacrifice to God.

#53 = 1 Peter **5:3** NLT
Don't lord it over the people assigned to your care, but lead them by your own good example.

#54 1 John **5:4** NLT
 For every child of God defeats this evil world, and we achieve this victory through our faith.

#55 = 1 John **5:5** NLT
And who can win this battle against the world? Only those who believe that Jesus is the Son of God.

#56 = 1 Peter **5:6** NIV
Humble yourselves, therefore, under God's mighty hand, that he may lift you up in due time.

#57 = 1 Peter **5:7** NIV
Cast all your anxiety on him because he cares for you.

#58 = Ephesians **5:8** NLT
For once you were full of darkness, but now you have light from the Lord. So live as people of light!

#59 = 1 Peter **5:9** NLT
Stand firm against him, and be strong in your faith. Remember that your family of believers all over the world is going through the same kind of suffering you are.

#60 = Isaiah **60**:1 NLT
""Arise, Jerusalem! Let your light shine for all to see. For the glory of the LORD rises to shine on you."

#61 = Hebrews **6:1** NLT
So let us stop going over the basic teachings about Christ again and again. Let us go on instead and become mature in our understanding. Surely we don't need to start again with the fundamental importance of repenting from evil deeds and placing our faith in God.

#62 = Galatians **6:2** NIV
Carry each other's burdens, and in this way you will fulfill the law of Christ.

#63 = 2 Corinthians **6:3** NLT
We live in such a way that no one will stumble because of us, and no one will find fault with our ministry.

#64 = Romans **6:4** NLT
For we died and were buried with Christ by baptism. And just as Christ was raised from the dead by the glorious power of the Father, now we also may live new lives.

#65 = Deuteronomy **6:5** NLT
And you must love the Lord your God with all your heart, all your soul, and all your strength.

#66 = 1 Timothy **6:6** NIV
But godliness with contentment is great gain.

#67 = Galatians **6:7** NIV
Do not be deceived: God cannot be mocked. A man reaps what he sows.

#68 = Isaiah **6:8** NIV
Then I heard the voice of the Lord saying, "Whom shall I send? And who will go for us?" And I said, "Here am I. Send me!"

#69 = Galatians **6:9** NLT
So let's not get tired of doing what is good. At just the right time we will reap a harvest of blessing if we don't give up.

#70 = Psalms **70**:4 NLT
But may all who search for you be filled with joy and gladness in you. May those who love your salvation repeatedly shout, "God is great!"

Jersey Number Bible Verses

#71 = 2 Corinthians **7:1** NIV
Therefore, since we have these promises, dear friends, let us purify ourselves from everything that contaminates body and spirit, perfecting holiness out of reverence for God.

#72 = Proverbs **7:2** NLT
Obey my commands and live! Guard my instructions as you guard your own eyes.

#73 = Proverbs **7:3** NLT
Tie them on your fingers as a reminder. Write them deep within your heart.

#74 = 2 Corinthians **7:4** NIV
I have spoken to you with great frankness; I take great pride in you. I am greatly encouraged; in all our troubles my joy knows no bounds.

#75 = Ecclesiastes **7:5** NLT
Better to be criticized by a wise person than to be praised by a fool.

#76 = 2 Corinthians **7:6** NLT
But God, who encourages those who are discouraged, encouraged us by the arrival of Titus.

#77 = Matthew **7:7** NIV
"Ask and it will be given to you; seek and you will find; knock and the door will be opened to you.

#78 = Matthew **7:8** NLT
For everyone who asks, receives. Everyone who seeks, finds. And to everyone who knocks, the door will be opened.

#79 = Isaiah **7:9**b NIV
If you do not stand firm in your faith, you will not stand at all.' "

#80 = Psalms **80**:7 NLT
"Turn us again to yourself, O God of Heaven's Armies. Make your face shine down upon us. Only then will we be saved."

#81 = Romans **8:1** NIV
Therefore, there is now no condemnation for those who are in Christ Jesus,

#82 = Romans **8:2** NLT
And because you belong to him, the power of the life-giving Spirit has freed you from the power of sin that leads to death.

#83 = 1 Corinthians **8:3** NLT
But the person who loves God is the one whom God recognizes.

#**84** = Psalm **8:4** NIV
what is mankind that you are mindful of them, human beings that you care for them?

#**85** = Romans **8:5** NIV
Those who live according to the flesh have their minds set on what the flesh desires; but those who live in accordance with the Spirit have their minds set on what the Spirit desires.

#**86** = Romans **8:6** NLT
So letting your sinful nature control your mind leads to death. But letting the Spirit control your mind leads to life and peace.

#**87** = Job **8:7** NLT
And though you started with little, you will end with much.

#**88** = Luke **8:8** NIV
Still other seed fell on good soil. It came up and yielded a crop, a hundred times more than was sown." When he said this, he called out, "Whoever has ears to hear, let them hear."

#**89** = Romans **8:9** NLT
But you are not controlled by your sinful nature. You are controlled by the Spirit if you have the Spirit of God living in you. (And remember that those who do not have the Spirit of Christ living in them do not belong to him at all.)

#**90** = Psalms **90**:2 NLT
"Before the mountains were born, before you gave birth to the earth and the world, from beginning to end, you are God."

#**91** = Psalms **9:1** NLT
I will praise you, Lord, with all my heart; I will tell of all the marvelous things you have done.

#**92** = Psalms **9:2** NLT
I will be filled with joy because of you. I will sing praises to your name, O Most High.

#**93** = John **9:3** NLT
"It was not because of his sins or his parents' sins," Jesus answered. "This happened so the power of God could be seen in him.

#94 = Daniel **9:4** NLT
I prayed to the Lord my God and confessed: "O Lord, you are a great and awesome God! You always fulfill your covenant and keep your promises of unfailing love to those who love you and obey your commands.

#95 =John **9:5** NLT
But while I am here in the world, I am the light of the world."

#96 = Isaiah **9:6** NLT
 For a child is born to us, a son is given to us. The government will rest on his shoulders. And he will be called: Wonderful Counselor, Mighty God, Everlasting Father, Prince of Peace.

#97 = 2 Corinthians **9:7** NLT
You must each decide in your heart how much to give. And don't give reluctantly or in response to pressure. "For God loves a person who gives cheerfully."

#98 = Proverbs **9:8** NLT
So don't bother correcting mockers; they will only hate you. But correct the wise, and they will love you.

#99 = Daniel **9:9** NLT
But the Lord our God is merciful and forgiving, even though we have rebelled against him.

I Dedicate This Book To You...

Calista Danielle Priscilla Tadeo Wickert

Looking back on the date 9/19/2012 brings me to tears when I really think about what happened that day when I first met you at our 8:30 p.m. yard sale Emily Grace wanted to have. My world was changed forever after that day, not knowing in the moment that you were going to be a new addition to my family. I know I push you to be the best you can be and I really do love hanging out with you. I believe God was showing off when he made you! You're so beautiful, smart, and gifted in tons of areas! You have an amazing sense of humor that I love to be around. Some of my favorite memories together are watching really dumb, but funny movies and quoting funny lines all day long. I know I wasn't there for your birth, but I was there for your spiritual birth when you got baptized. I was honored to baptize you into the family of Christ. Thanks for choosing me to baptize you and to be the father figure in your life. I'll never forget when you memorized James chapter One and we quoted that together with those big gold chains on.

I might have missed the first eleven years of your life, but I'll spend the next 100 years, if I can, loving on you and teaching you everything I know about seeking Jesus first, so you can have the most blessed life possible. I might be your stepdad, but I hope I've been a step up from what you expected in a stepdad. God never makes mistakes and I know God brought us together to wreck this world for Jesus together till the day we die. Ky, I want to dedicate this song to you as our song, "The One You Need" by the band Shane & Shane. Every time I hear it, I think of you. Please, look it up, and if something ever happens to me, just imagine me singing this song to you.

I'm proud to call you my daughter and thank you for accepting me as your dad. We might be a blended family, but we are a blessed one at that, thanks to seeking Jesus first!

The Bible verse I want to dedicate to you is 3 John 1:4 (NIV): **"I have no greater joy than to hear that my children are walking in the truth."** Ky always run after the Truth of God, He will never fail you when you seek Him with your whole heart, I promise.

Emily Grace Wickert,

I remember the first breath you ever took on 5/24/07 at 3:53 p.m. It was love at first sight. When I got to hold you for the first time, I truly understood what the meaning of unconditional love was. I thought I knew what true love was before, but it wasn't until I held you in my arms for the first time that God revealed it to me. Emily Grace, you are so amazing and I believe God would have won the 1st place prize for Most Beautiful Child the day He made you. You are so pretty, funny, confident, and have an amazing sense of humor! You are so talented in many areas of life. I'm so blessed to be your dad. I see a lot of myself in you and it's my biggest honor to be your Daddy. I've loved every minute of your life, from watching you take your first steps, to you throwing up in my hands during a church service at CCV (LOL). It's going to be exciting to see where Jesus takes you, girl, and I can't wait to walk you down the aisle one day when you meet that godly man we've been praying for at bedtime.

I chose your middle name Grace after the Bible verse Ephesians 2:8 (NIV): **"For it is by grace you have been saved, through faith—and this is not from yourselves, it is the gift of God."** I pray you never forget the amazing grace of God in your life and I pray that Jesus continues to grow and grow your understanding what grace truly is. Just like God's grace in my life, Emily, you are an amazing gift that I did not deserve.

Dedication

Emily Grace, I want to dedicate this song to you as our song called, "Find Your Wings" by Mark Harris. Every time I hear it I think of you. Please, look up this song and if something ever happens to me just imagine me singing this song to you. As you like to say Emily, I love you as BIG AS JESUS!

Andrew James Wickert,
Andrew, you probably won't get a chance to read this on this side of heaven, but I love you so much it hurts! You're priceless, son, and you mean the world to me! I know Jesus has a plan for your life and you bring joy to everyone that meets you. I know you can't pick a favorite Bible verse so I picked one out for you that you live out every day. Nehemiah 8:10 (NIV) says, "**for the joy of the Lord is your strength!**" Wow, you really do live this out son. You have so much joy and love for others! I love hearing you laugh and cry because your "Cars" movie is over and you want me to restart it. I hope Jesus lets you stay with us for many more years. Every night I tuck you in bed I whisper to you, "If you happen to go to heaven tonight, please tell Jesus I said hi and give Him a big hug for me." Andrew, I can't wait to hang out in heaven with you and Jesus and play ping-pong with golden paddles. I'm so proud to be your father. I hope you've enjoyed me as your Daddy.

Andrew James Wickert, I want to dedicate this song to you as our song called "How Great is Our God" by Chris Tomlin. Every time I hear it I think of you, son. I pray this song over you and proclaim it in Jesus Name!

Hope Saphire Wickert,
Words can't express how thankful I am to God that He you to us. **"Every time I think of you, I give thanks to my God"** Philippians 1:3 (NLT). You're beautiful red hair and contagious smile makes my day brighter every time I see you. I remember the

241

exact date of 12/2 and the feeling I had when we first found out we were having you! I believe when you were born, you turned our blended family into a blessed family forever. You brought unity to our families and made it one. I know Jesus was showing off when He made you.

 I named this ministry after you, Hope, and Jesus told me that as you grow, it is how this ministry is going to grow. I hope one day you'll take over this ministry and bless your kids with it. I named you after this Bible verse Jeremiah 29:11 "'For I know the plans I have for you,' declares the Lord, 'plans to prosper you and not to harm you, plans to give you HOPE and a future.'" WOW, did that verse become so true for us! Hope, you mean the world to your mom and me. We can't wait to see the plans Jesus has for you! I know you're going to wreck this world for Jesus till the day you die with me!

 Hope Saphire Wickert, I want to dedicate this song to you as our song called "Only Hope" by Switchfoot. I used to dance around the kitchen with you snuggled in my arms and sing this song to you! Please, look up this song when you are old enough and if anything ever happens to me just know I am singing this song over you with Jesus in Heaven.

Made in the USA
Middletown, DE
14 November 2023